Religions of the East

Lucius Boraks, CFX

Sheed & Ward

Sheed & Ward™ is a service of National Catholic Reporter Publishing Company, Inc.

ISBN: 1-55612-140-7

Published by: Sheed & Ward
                115 E. Armour Blvd. P.O. Box 414292
                Kansas City, MO 64141-4292

To order, call: (800) 333-7373

Contents

Introduction

In the Letter to the Hebrews we read, "At various times in the past and in various different ways, God spoke to our ancestors..." (Hebrews 1:1). "At various times and in various ways," that is what this book is all about. Just how did God "speak" to our ancestors? How did God make an abiding presence known in creation? It is an attempt to penetrate the varied manifestations of this Presence in the world and the religious sensitivities in humanity that helped make them aware of this Presence. The first part of our search will take us back to primitive human beings in the belief that religion is as old as humanity itself. We will try to understand the nature and origins of religion: what leads people to a religious awareness, what experiences may have revealed the godhead to them, how did humans first express their religious convictions, and how did religious beliefs affect their daily life. We will examine the notion that the different ways that primitive religions perceived the reality of the world of the sacred reflected in large measure the cultural background of those societies.

The bulk of this study will revolve around the origins and ideas of the world's major living religions of the eastern half of the world. In India we will find four major faiths of varying degrees of antiquity: the very ancient, even timeless Hinduism, then the contemporary reform movements of the enormously popular Buddhism, together with the somewhat more ascetical Jainism, and lastly the curious and almost modern faith of the Sikhs with its heavy political undertones. Next we will focus on the religions native to China, Confucianism and Taoism, each with roots that may even antedate Hinduism. Then we turn to Japan and the Shinto faith with all its ambiguities and complexities. Buddhism too has a place among the oriental religions, and so we will look at one of its most successful forms, Zen Buddhism. We will then move to the Middle-East to examine Zoroastrianism, and try to determine what if any effect it may have had on the more enduring and influential parent religion of Christianity, namely Judaism. Finally we will attempt to understand the Jewish faith and the role that it played as a kind of a "bridge" between eastern and western religions.

Perhaps we should admit at the very outset a certain bias or perspective that we share as Christians, and that this is bound to color our perception of the great religions of the world. We will be seeing them through Christian eyes, for the rest of that quotation from Hebrews runs, "but in our own time, the last days, He has spoken to us through His Son..." (Hebrews 1:2). It is not our intention to offer the reader a kind of smorgasbord of religious ideas from which to pick and choose that which for whatever reason appeals to him. Rather it is our hope and stated intention to strengthen and deepen the reader's own Christian commitment through an appreciation of the religious perceptions of other peoples. We believe that God has spoken to these peoples "in various ways" and that he has revealed to them some very wonderful truths both about Himself and about our common human nature (see the Vatican II document entitled *Declaration on the Relation of the Church to Non-Christian Religions*, #2). Through this study we hope to learn some of those truths.

Many of the religions we will be considering present a number of important truths for our reflection. One thinks of the beauty, simplicity, and remarkable detachment from material things so characteristic of the religions of India. The profound respect for life these eastern religions exhibit, the love and kinship they feel for nature, and the devotion and prayerfulness with which they live out each day—all of these things command our respect and admiration. We can learn much about human values from them. Prepare to be inspired.

Lastly, our approach is based on the conviction that the whole gamut of world religions reveals a provident, loving God—the same God we have come to know as Christians, the God who guides all of His creation into His fatherly embrace. One principle should become apparent: the story of religion is as varied and complex as the character of human nature in which it has been manifested.

The Nature Of Religion

Religion Is As Old As Humanity

A question that is often asked by students is, "When did religion begin?" or "How long has man been religious?" The honest answer to those questions is, of course, "No one really knows for certain." And yet one can theorize. One theory suggests that religion is as old as man himself. There seems to be ample evidence at least confirming this possibility. Archeologists, that is, scientists who study the very earliest signs of human life on our planet, report finding evidence again and again among fossil remains for man's concern about what one might call "the sacred." Concern about death and what follows death, the use of ritual to gain power to deal with the challenges of daily living, signs and symbols of concerns over taboos and forbidden actions, evidence of a belief in a spirit-world, preservation of sacred stories—all these abound among evidence of primitive lives.

Science And The Origins Of The Human Race How Old Is Humanity?		
Time Span	**Era**	**Life-Forms**
4-2.5 billion	Archeozoic	No Life On Earth
2.5-1 billion	Proterozoic	Plant Life, Fish
1 b. -300 million	Paleozoic	Amphibians, Reptiles
300-150 million	Mesozoic	Mammals begin to appear
150-1 million	Cenozoic	The Age of Mammals
1 m. to present	Pleistocene	Human-like creatures and Human Beings

The Pleistocene Era		
Time Span	**Period**	**Dominant Species**
1 m. -500,000	Early Pleistocene	Human-like Creatures Appear
500,000-present	Late Pleistocene	Humans may have appeared and coexisted with Human-like creatures
500,000-200,000	Early Paleolithic	Pithecanthropus (China) Australopithecus (Java) Zinjanthropus (Africa) along with many others
200,000-40,000	Middle Paleolithic	Cromagnon and Neanderthal
40,000-13,000	Late Paleolithic	Modern Human Beings
13,000-5,000	Mesolithic	
5,000-present	Historic	

But how long ago was that? How long has man walked the earth? There are no definite answers to that question yet. In the last hundred years or so a great deal has been learned about human origins and the origins of the earth itself. Today most scientists put the age of the earth at about four and a half billion years. The possibility of human life, scientists tell us, came quite a bit later, certainly no earlier than a million years ago. In fact, if one were to compare the total age of the earth to a single calendar year, man would not appear until late on the last day of the year, perhaps just a few minutes before midnight on December 31st.

What About Evolution?

Christians, who firmly believe in God's creative act which called everything that is into being, like to explain the gap between the creation of the earth and that of man as the long period of preparation which God deemed neccessary for man's entrance into the world. Although it really is not the purpose of this book to develop a scientific explanation for the origins of the human race, nevertheless this text does follow an evolutionary approach in these matters, and generally presumes that religion evolved, along with everything else.

Christians may believe in the theory of evolution, as a most plausible explanation for the wonder of creation and even of man himself, so long as they continue to hold that God created man directly at a given moment in time, endowing him with a spirit manifested in intelligence and free will. Mainline Christians have little difficulty in this area because, unlike fundamentalists, they do not find it neccessary to defend the historical time-frame or sequence of creation presented in the Book of Genesis. They believe that the Bible can be held to be true and without error with regard to the religious truths that it presents, quite apart from its concept of history and science: they honor the Bible as a record of divine revelation, God speaking to people, in terms of religious truths alone.

The creation account in Genesis suggests that God revealed himself directly to our first parents at the very beginning (*genesis*) of their existence. And yet one may suppose that our first parents may well have received this revelation through very ordinary means. Here cultural anthropologists, that is, scientists who study primitive human behavior, as well as historians of religion, often conjecture that this revelation of man's relationship to his creator may have been discovered quite naturally. If one defines religion as "a consciousness of one's relationship to one's creator," then perhaps the distinction made between a sibling (brother-sister) and a spousal (husband-wife) relationship can be helpful. The spousal relationship is one that requires some effort to establish, whereas the sibling relationship is one that comes naturally, one is simply born into it. One theory regarding the origin of religion is that it simply comes naturally; one is born into it.

The Dawn Of Religious Consciousness

This understanding in no way compromises the religious truths found in Genesis, since the religious truth taught in that account is very simple: God created man and woman directly, and placed them at the pinnacle of His created world, giving them dominion over all other creatures. The human author of this story chose a more dramatic way to express this particular inspired truth, namely that God revealed Himself directly to them and made them aware of their relationship to Him, as creatures to their Creator. We are free to explain this awareness in a less dramatic and more realistic and natural manner.

This dawning of religious consciousness may have evolved more slowly, and in any number of ways. Primitive man may have gradually become aware of another whole order of being through his every day experiences. He probably enjoyed a much more finely tuned sensitivity to the world of the sacred than do moderns. He may have regarded many of his experiences as more meaningful. Somewhat as a child, who is continuously discovering new experiences, the primitive discovered and sought meaning for functions that he valued as vital to his existence. This notion of "the sacred" therefore may be defined as that level of human experience that is considered quite apart from the ordinary or profane, an experience that is full of meaning and ultimate value. Primitives, who were after all gifted with the same intellectual powers that moderns are, could have reasoned to the possibility of another whole order of existence which utterly transcended their own through the very ordinary means of their own participation in these "sacred functions."

One can only imagine the variety of venues through which this "revelation" might have been received. It is important to remember that primitives lived an almost child-like existence: they had no formal education, were not scientific, and were probably impressed very easily by things they could not explain. With this in mind, imagine the impact dreams might have had. Today there is a scientific explanation for this psychological phenomenon, and yet to primitives dreams might have seemed quite eerie. Friends and relations long dead could appear and even communicate with the living. This may have strongly suggested to the primitive that there is continued existence after death and another world of the spirits. There are numerous instances in the Bible in which dreams are the occasions of divine messages. Even to the Hebrews dreams were valued as opportunities to participate in the world of the sacred.

In primitive man's endless struggle with nature one can imagine still another venue. Primitives were in many ways victims of their environment: heat, cold, drought, flood, availability of food—all these things were in the "hands" of nature, and nature could be very fickle. Could this reality have led to a personification of this powerful force in man's life? Nature might be perceived as kind or cruel, generous or stingy—all animate, personal qualities. Was this control over man's fortunes then seen as a sacred power? To the primitive surrounded as he was by superior and unseen forces, this conclusion might have appeared as inescapable. In fact anthropologists who have studied primitive cultures still found in some parts of the world have made the same observations.

Sacred Time And Sacred Space

The twin dimensions of human existence are time and space. Whatever human beings do, at least in the earthly phase of their lives, is conditioned by one or both of these limitations. As a matter of fact, the negation of time and space is often the way the perfection of the after-life is described, as in the concept of "eternity" which is the never-ending, eternally present state of the blessed. Primitives too may have reasoned to the possibility of this ideal state, since they too felt the limitations on their lives imposed by time and space. It is not surprising then that primitives could have projected an idealized existence on which no such constraints were placed.

In terms of time, many primitives conceived of a time apart from profane or ordinary time, a sacred time. Frequently this was understood as "a time before time," or a beginning time. Those who were fortunate enough to live at this time, since they were able to live free of these twin limitations, were considered "gods," and their actions models of idealized human behavior. This notion gave rise, scholars believe, to what is known as mythology, stories which embodied the projections of a people's ideals. These stories were composed to represent to the community, especially to the young, the way the most important, most meaningful actions in life ought to be performed. They were concerned that actions this important be done "the right way." Myths were the rubrics, the models that one needed to follow to be certain things were done right. Myths came to be employed as the expressions of a people's most treasured ideals, their creeds, as it were. Myths, in fact, are of their very nature religious statements since they most often deal with a particular culture's idea of the sacred.

Mircea Eliade, a famous historian of religions, suggests that mythology became for primitives the key to experiencing the sacred. He found in his research a wealth of evidence connecting the celebration of religious festivals with the temporary escape from the mundane conditions of time and space, leading to the consequent experience of a higher level of existence which he calls "the sacred." In these festivals man, by ritually reenacting those model actions of "the gods" described in the myths, in a sense became those gods and thus entered the world of the sacred. Bronislaw Malinowski, another anthropoligist specializing in the study of primitive cultures, after years of observations made in the islands of Oceania, came up with essentially the same conclusions regarding the use of myths among primitives.

Festivals

Festivals were then the occasions used by primitives to experience the liberating effects of sacred time. Most primitive cultures had an altogether different approach to time than do moderns. For moderns, time is linear, a sequence of moments rushing past, never to be recaptured. The poet laments, "The sands of time wait for no man." Time is irreversible. For most primitives, however, this was not the way they looked at time. They perceived time as cyclical, cycles of time beginning, running their course, ending, and then beginning all over again. Time therefore repeated itself endlessly, like so many other things in their human experience: the seasons of the year, the days and nights, the vegetation around them, even the life cycle itself. Primitives, living at a much slower pace than do moderns, might logically presume pauses between the cycles of time, pauses that constitute a kind of "time before time." The Babylonian New Year festival, for example, lasted ten days. All through that ten days time was sacred, not profane. These days were not even counted as part of the calendar year. There was a total suspension of all profane activities. Everything, every action, every person existed, for a time at least, in the world of the sacred, enjoying a unique experience free of all the many limitations of ordinary (profane) human existence.

During these festivals the actions of the gods (those who lived in the time before time, at the beginning) presented in the myths were dramatically reenacted. By doing so the primitives in a sense became the gods themselves. This is not as far-fetched as it sounds, and should not be a concept foreign to the Judaeo-Christian tradition of festivals. Think, for example, of the Jewish observance of the Sabbath. What is being celebrated? The first Sabbath or seventh day of creation. How is it celebrated? The Jews do what God did on that first of Sabbaths: they reenact that beginning time by refraining from all labor, just as God rested from His labor of the creation. And the same principle applies to their celebration of Passover. Jews all over the world on that day do exactly what their ancestors did in Egypt prior to their deliverance from bondage. They reenact that sacred meal taken in haste following to the letter the strict directions God gave Moses. By doing so, each Jew since that sacred time has identified himself with those present at "the beginning" and shares in the liberating experience of the Exodus.

With Christian festivals it is much the same. In their celebration of the sacraments, Christians reenact certain life-giving actions of Christ and union with Christ, either establishing that union for the first time, as in baptism and confirmation, or reestablishing it as in reconcilation, or affirming and nourishing it in some way as with all the other sacraments. In the Eucharist, for example, Christians share the bread and cup, just as Christ did at the Last Supper, anticipating His own saving death. By so doing, each Christian believes he is affirming his union with Christ at the most perfect moment of His entire earthly life, as He offered to His Heavenly Father the perfect sacrifice of His life to save us all. Time in the ordinary sense ceases to limit one, for one is right there at the foot of the cross—in mystery.

Manifestations Of The Sacred

Over the course of the history of religions, different peoples have perceived the sacred manifesting itself in different ways. Some religions conceived the sacred present throughout creation, in every aspect of life: not only in living beings, but even in what moderns would consider inanimate things like mountains, streams, the sun and the stars. Primitives were not so sure they were inanimate. This belief that everything is sacred is called *pantheism*. Other peoples, or sometimes the same people at a different time, limited the presence of the sacred to certain powerful, living beings—but not all. This belief is *polytheism*. Some religions have seen the sacred present in two equal but opposite beings, one good and the other evil. This is *dualism*. Finally, some religions have understood the sacred to exist in one and only one being. This, of course, is *monotheism*. In this survey of world religions examples of each of these different views will be covered.

The Evolution Of Religious Systems

Experts in the history of religions have an interesting theory with regard to the variety of perceptions of the sacred, a theory which is based on evolution. They suggest that studies show that the most primitive societies known have been pantheistic. More advanced cultures seemed to adopt polytheistic views, seeing the sacred limited to a few powerful beings or gods. They note a transition from pantheism to polytheism which seems to arise from certain distinctions often found in pantheistic systems. *Animism* is a pantheistic belief in the spirit-world, based on the concept that every being has a spirit or animating force. But where does this life-giving spirit originate? Polytheism provided an answer to this fundamental question by affirming the existence of an animator or spirit-giver. This not only creates a hierarchy among sacred beings, some dependent on others, but also accepts the notion of limitation, that is the idea that some beings are less sacred than others, and some not sacred at all. Hence the existence of some privileged, unlimited beings or gods, such as one finds in polytheistic religions. The other transitional step from pantheism to polytheism may have been the belief in naturism, or the idea that focuses on nature as the principal expression of the sacred. Primitives, who were in awe of nature, may have reasoned that, since in their struggle with the forces of nature and their environment they were often victims rather than victors, these superior forces ought to be worshipped. Thus the polytheistic gods so common in primitive religions.

Another explanation for the apparent evolution in religious systems rests on one of the most perplexing issues that man has ever faced—the problem of evil. Why do evil things happen? And more confounding, why do evil things happen to good people? Primitive polytheistic pantheons usually included evil gods as well as good ones, and perhaps this was the way the problem of evil was explained. While good things happened due to the generosity of the good gods, evil things were caused by the malice of evil gods. Primitives were apt to attribute everything that happened to them to some action of the gods. Moderns, of course, have the scientific view that, although God may be the ultimate cause of everything, nevertheless there are always more direct causes to be considered. This in fact is what science is all about: the study of secondary causality. Primitives, however, by definition are not scientific.

In some religious systems the causes of good and evil were seen as opposite principles or beings who alone controlled man's fate. When things were going well, it was the good god who deserved the credit, but when things went badly, the blame was put on the evil god. Curiously both gods were worshipped: the good god out of gratitude, the evil out of fear, in the hope that he might be placated. Christians are often equally puzzled by the problem of evil, and try to explain it by admitting that evil is simply one of life's many mysteries. For dualists, evil was no mystery. They had a very logical explanation for it.

Three Early Mediterranean Religions

Three very different approaches to the world of the sacred may be found among the early civilizations of the eastern Mediterranean. In recent years archeologists have learned a great deal about these cultures. They are the Babylonians, the Egyptians, and the Greeks. The three religions which these civilizations embraced were quite different. Modern psychology may throw some light on this disparity. Behavioral scientists suggest that the way each person perceives God is often dependent on one's background, upbringing, and family life. For example, a person who did not enjoy a warm and loving relationship with his or her parents as a child may be incapable of relating to God as a loving parent. What applies to individuals, they argue, may also apply to whole cultures.

The Babylonian gods were fearsome: strong, willful, jealous, demanding, constantly at odds with one another. Tension and conflict colored the atmosphere that pervaded the world of their deities. Could the reason the Babylonians perceived their gods in this manner be the fact that life for them was not so easy? They lived in a valley between the Tigris and the Euphrates Rivers, known today as Iraq. These inhabitants of this desert area had to struggle to stay alive. The land was not very fertile, and agricultural success depended solely on the flooding of the rivers each spring. Hostile neighbors kept them always on the defensive. Did their vision of life itself color their vision of the world of the sacred?

Life was quite pleasant for the Egyptians. They lived then, as they do now, for the most part within ten miles on each side of the great Nile River, whose life-giving and life-sustaining waters provided an abundance of the good things in life. The nation grew strong, and it seldom suffered from fear of invasion and conquest by other peoples. The Egyptians were grateful to their gods as benevolent, loving deities who promised an after-life of joy and plenty.

With the Greeks one finds a kind of middle ground. They also enjoyed a bountiful life: the sun was warm, the sea provided fish, the rich soil yielded olives and grapes as well as other staple crops. The Greeks flourished and generated a culture perhaps unequalled for its quality of life both of the body and the spirit. The Greeks had developed a remarkable degree of philosophical insight and self-awareness. Apparently they felt little need to credit the gods for their good fortune, for the gods they imagined populating Mount Olympus were quite independent and aloof, totally unconcerned with the mere mortals dwelling below. They were perceived as proud, petty, jealous of one another's powers, and completely occupied with themselves. Again religious attitudes seem to have been formed as a reflection of a cultural bias.

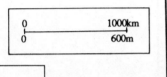

Earliest centers of civilization

Earliest Civilizations, 3500-1000 B.C.E.

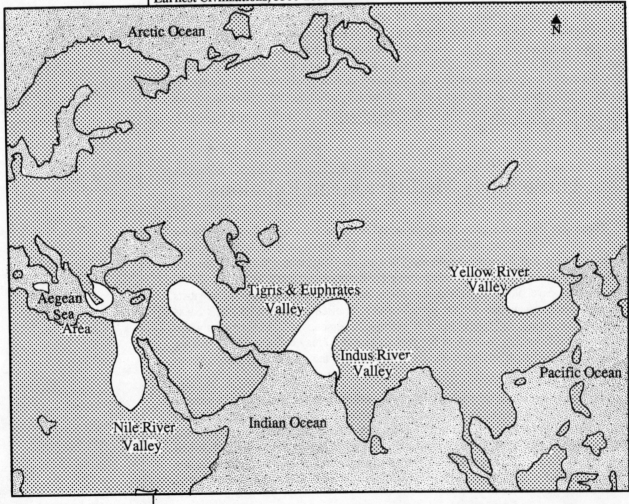

The Origins Of Monotheism

According to this theory that religious systems evolved just lke everything else, a similar transition may have occurred between polytheism and monotheism. In many polytheistic religions, the Greeks for example, there is found the belief that among the many gods one is supreme. This concept is called *monarchianism,* obviously deriving its name from the idea of a king-god. In some instances this one supreme god becomes the only true god, the others being relegated to the status of minor deities or in some few cases angels. It is interesting to note that the word for god in Hebrew is *El* while the word for angels is *elohim* or "little gods." This same notion of gods being demoted to angelic status seems to have occurred in Islam with its thousands of *jini.*

Another variation on polytheism which may have been instrumental in the evolution of monotheism is *monolatry,* which is the belief in many gods, but the worship of only one. This idea may have been worked out quite logically, once again because of the primitive's belief in primary causality. He may have reasoned that battles were won or lost depending on whose god was stronger. And yet he was faithful to this god no matter what. Though his enemy's god may be real, it was not his god. This expression of monolatrous polytheism occurs again and again in the Hebrew Scriptures which pre-date the Exile. The First Commandment may not have been so much a command to monotheism as it was to monolatry: "I am the Lord, your God; you shall have no gods except me" (Exodus 20:1f). In fact biblical scholars believe that the Jews came to their belief in pure monotheism only gradually.

This evolutionary approach to the history of religions is of course only a theory, but it is a theory that is based on a great deal of evidence which makes it quite plausible that monotheism is the end-product of a long line of religious evolution. Many of the earliest examples of monotheism which appeared briefly in certain cultures may have developed similarly. The New World Indians, both in North and Central America, the Asian Indians, and even the Egyptians all seem to have embraced at least temporarily this kind of primitive monotheism.

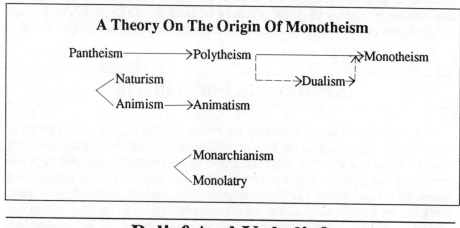

A Theory On The Origin Of Monotheism

Pantheism ——————→ Polytheism ┌————————→ Monotheism

Naturism

Animism ———→ Animatism └----→ Dualism →

Monarchianism

Monolatry

Belief And Unbelief

It might appear that all people down through the ages possess a religious consciousness, that this comes quite naturally to everyone. But this is not necessarily true. It may be said that religious consciousness is a universal human phenomenon, but this must be understood to mean that religion may be found everywhere, in every age, and among every people. It is quite possible for individuals not to believe, not to be religious.

This question of unbelief is very important. Christians sometimes take their ability to believe for granted. It ought to be remembered that faith, defined simply as the ability to believe, to be religious, is a gift from God—a gift not everyone shares. Faith must be a gift from above because without it one could not possibly believe all the things one is asked to believe. There is a good reason for this. The act of belief is but one of several different acts the intellect is capable of performing. Normally the intellect follows certain guidelines. For example, when the intellect renders assent to a particular proposition, it does so because it has convincing proof of the truth of that proposition. Likewise when the intellect denies assent, it does so because there is no proof for that proposition. In both assent and dissent the intellect acts out of conviction.

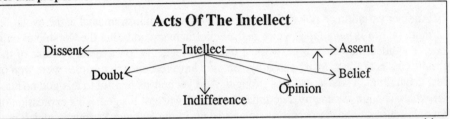

Acts Of The Intellect

With regard to the act of belief, the intellect does render total assent to a proposition of faith, as for example the existence of God, but it does so without proof. No one can prove that God exists; one believes that He exists. And yet belief is an act of the intellect. But how or why does the intellect act in defiance of its own guidelines? The only answer that can be given to that question is this. The grace of God's gift of faith moves the intellect to give total assent in the absence of proof. Without this gift of faith and the grace that makes it possible, the intellect would withold its assent to any proposition of faith. This is what the atheist must do.

An atheist is one who denies God's existence. That is not the same as the agnostic, who denies only that he knows for certain whether God exists, and takes no steps to settle the question. An agnostic neither affirms nor denies God's existence. He is indifferent to the proposition, and in that sense is more to be pitied than the atheist. Many atheists attempt to justify their lack of faith by attacking those who do believe. It would be wise to be familiar with some of the more common arguments heard from atheists.

Arguments For Atheism

One of the most common arguments for atheism is what might be called the sociological theory. Some atheists are fond of deriding religion as a hoax. Man made God, they say, rather than the other way around. Society has created God or gods for men to revere as a way of controlling human behavior. They might argue, for example, that Moses did not receive the Ten Commandments in a mystical experience atop Mount Sinai, but that he made them up himself to impose law and order on the unruly and uncooperative Hebrew Tribes as they made their way to the Promised Land. In short, man uses religion to control his fellow man.

Another argument rests on what might be called a Freudian theory. Sigmund Freud, the father of moder psychiatry, believed that religion is a crutch needed only by the weak in order to cope with frustration and guilt. Those who are psychologically mature have no such need and, in fact, would be better off without religion, which can inhibit true growth and independence.

Still other atheists argue from a scientific base. They believe that modern science now supplies the answers to life's mysteries, answers once only religion could provide. The theory of evolution, they say, answers any question one might have about the origin of the universe. The concept of a loving, personal God who creates and sustains the world no longer is needed. In fact man's need for God diminishes in proportion to the growth in the body of scientific knowledge.

Finally, there are atheists who like to argue from moral grounds. The problem of evil, they suggest, should prevent any rational person from believing in God. If God does exist, and He is all-loving and all-powerful, then how or why would He allow evil to exist in the world? But evil does exist, and good people do suffer, so God must not exist.

The Christian's Response

The author of Hebrews reminds us, "Only faith can guarantee the blessings we hope for, or prove the existence of the realities that at present are unseen" (Hebrews 11:1). These arguments, so convincing to the atheist, carry little weight with the believer. There are, of course, a number of Christian responses that might be made to them, but they would probably not impress an atheist. One recalls a line from Franz Werfel's *Song of Bernadette,* in which he is speaking of the miraculous cures at Lourdes, which goes, "To the believer no explanation is necessary; to the non-believer no explanation is possible!"

What then should the believer's attitude be toward the atheist? The Church teaches that, provided he or she is following his or her conscience, the atheist, too, may be saved since no more can be expected of any human being. This teaching on religious freedom and the obligation each person has to follow his conscience—a teaching which emphasizes the gratuity of the gift of faith—was reiterated in this century in Vatican II's *Declaration on Religious Liberty.* As for the agnostic, one can only leave him to God's mercy.

Questions For Review

1. Describe an experience you have had with "the sacred." This may have occurred in one or more of several contexts, such as nature, friendship, sorrow, joy, "mystery," death or near-death, but do not use those which may have happened in any religious context.

2. Who would be more sensitive to experiences with the sacred, do you think, modern or pre-modern man, and why?

3. Trace the origins of monotheism, according to at least one theory.

4. Identify: sacred, profane, mythology, "idealized human behavior," linear time, sacred time, cyclical time, festival, primary causality, axis mundi, pantheism, animism, naturism, polytheism, dualism, monarchianism, monolatry, monotheism.

5. Compose a fictitious conversation between an atheist and a believer in which the most commonly heard arguments for and against the existence of God are rehearsed.

6. State four "common grounds" for atheism one encounters, and then give a typical Christian response to each of them.

7. According to the most recent teaching of the Catholic Church, what hope do atheists have for salvation?

8. Show how the act of belief differs radically from other intellectual acts. What does this distinction have to say about the Christian's attitude toward atheists?

9. Write a brief report about any three of these famous atheists or agnostics: Jean-Paul Sartre, Thomas Paine, Percy Blythe Shelly, Julian Huxley, Voltaire, Diderot, Lenin.

2

The Religions of India

"Verily, the soul is
Brahma,
made of knowledge,
of mind,
of breath,
of seeing,
of hearing,
of earth,
of water,
of wind,
of space,
of energy...
It is made of everything."

The Upanishads

The Hindus

Hinduism has been called the oldest living religion. Certainly its roots are very old indeed. Its antiquity may have something to do with the complexity of this ancient faith, but perhaps complexity is not so much the problem with grasping the essence of Hinduism so much as its diversity. If one could challenge Hinduism's claim to be the oldest of the world's religions, no one could doubt its title to the most diverse. In fact Hinduism has many faces. It is "all things to all men," not so much a single religious entity as an umbrella which shelters beneath its cover a whole panoply of religious ideas and expressions.

The Hindu Pantheon

The diversity which marks Hinduism begins with the Hindu notion of deity. There is a strange kind of unity in the vast multiplicity of the Hindu pantheon. One is never really certain whether the Hindu religion is pantheistic or polytheistic or dualistic or even monotheistic: there are indications that it is all of these—and none of these! In fact, many Hindus would have some difficulty addressing these categories at all. These terms, which westerners like to use to describe religious systems, just don't fit. They are merely ways to describe the Sacred, and in that limited sense these terms are all acceptable to the Hindu.

The Hindu notion of the sacred finds its broadest expression in Brahman, a term we might define as "sacredness itself," the very ground of all being, the common source of all of creation. Brahman is eternal, is changeless, has no equal, is fathomless and infinite—the ultimate reality. Brahman may be experienced only through its manifestations, through the world, which is a mere shadow of its reality. Brahman expresses itself in creation, brought into existence by Brahma the creator. Brahma is "the sacred one," the first of the personal manifestations of sacredness itself.

Although Hindus credit Brahma with the act of creation, he is not to be seen in the same terms that Christians use to appreciate their God because the differences are significant. For one thing Brahma creates but then seemingly abandons his creation to lesser gods and intercessors. He is like a "first act character" in a play, one who appears at the beginning of the drama but then disappears, and is not seen again until curtain call. This impersonal and somewhat aloof characteristic of Brahma suggests a kind of deism, the belief that one supreme God exists, has created the world, but has nothing to do with his creation. It also suggests a kind of monotheism of course, but again not like Judaeo-Christian monotheism.

The Hindu Trinity

As if to fill the need for a more personal deity, Hinduism provides other gods of a more personal nature. There are two major deities that all Hindus recognize, and yet not all worship. They are Vishnu, the Preserver, and Shiva, the Destroyer, who together with Brahma, the Creator, form a kind of trinity called the *trimurti*. These three gods are the principal manifestations of sacredness—Brahman. Because Vishnu

Shiva

and Shiva are of a somewhat opposite nature, one good and the other evil, there appears to be a kind of dualism in the Hindu faith as well. Vishnu, perhaps more than any other Hindu deity, approximates the Christian's God. Vishnu is kind, loving, merciful, even providential. The cult of Vishnu is found everywhere in India, and yet tends to be more popular with the urbanites. Shiva, on the other hand, is fearsome, cruel, fickle, even vindictive. The cult of Shiva again is found throughout India but principally with those who farm. Shiva is worshipped because it seems to pacify his destructive tendencies. The devotees of Vishnu proudly display painted on their foreheads two vertical stripes, while those of Shiva use two horizontal stripes to proclaim their loyalty.

But the manifestations or *avatars* of Brahman are not limited to the parts of the *trimurti* for all the gods of Hinduism are seen as expressions of the One, and they number in the thousands. Vishnu has nine different incarnations, including the well known Krishna and Rama. These two gods are extremely popular with Hindus and are the central characters in two very famous books in Hindu sacred literature. In addition to the avatars of Vishnu, Shiva is incarnate in a host of gods and goddesses, some in human forms and others in animal forms—most representing some aspect of fertility. As mentioned, all the many gods are considered to be manifestations of the sacred, and as such their number is not important: they are all simply the many faces of the One Reality, Brahman. Over thirty thousand gods have been identified, suggesting a religion best described as polytheistic, but in fact merely confirming an overwhelming sense of the presence of the sacred in every aspect of earthly life, a notion closer to pantheism than polytheism.

Not only do the gods and goddesses of Hinduism manifest Brahman. In a very real sense each individual is a part of the One. Hindus have another word for Brahman. It is *paramatman,* or the over-soul. And each individual possesses a soul, or *atman.* The spirit of each individual then shares in the One Reality of Brahman. In this view all of creation is sacred.

Vishnu

Hindu Sacred Literature

The Hindu religion, like the others in this survey, has its own sacred literature. Before looking at some examples, perhaps it would be wise to point out a very important distinction between sacred books in eastern religions as compared to western religions. In the major western religions—Judaism, Christianity, Islam—books are considered sacred because they have a Sacred Author. We call this notion *inspiration,* that is the belief that in these sacred books God is speaking to us through the human author, that somehow, some way, whatever the human author wrote was exactly what God wanted him to write. In every eastern religion in this study, this is not the case. These sacred books are considered sacred because they are about sacred things; they have a sacred subject-matter. There is no notion comparable to inspiration in eastern religions.

Just as the canon of Christian Scriptures would be two or three or more times the size it is were it not for the concept of inspiration, so too the collection of Hindu sacred books is quite large, and is defined differently by different scholars. For the purposes of this brief survey we are going to consider two categories of Hindu sacred literature: one comprising the most ancient and honored texts, containing some of the essential teachings of the religion, and the other made up of some very early but less doctrinal texts, texts which preserve much of the early mythology of the Indian people.

Indus Valley Civilization, 3000 B.C.E.-1000 C.E.

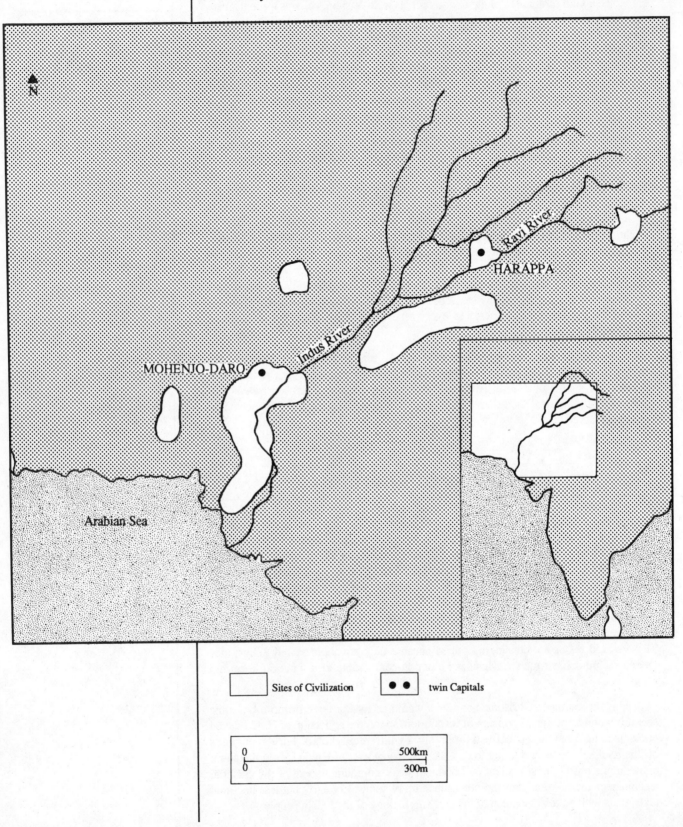

Sites of Civilization   ● ●   twin Capitals

The oldest of the Hindu sacred books is the *Vedas*. Beginning first as an oral tradition, the Vedas were first put down in writing around 1500 B.C. They contain hundreds of hymns, prayers, and ritual formularies whose origins more than likely predate any other known religion. The Vedas present a religious tradition populated with thousands of gods and heroes projecting the ideals of the people of Indus Valley. Incidentally, that is exactly how Hinduism gets its name. It is the religion of the people of the region of the Indus River, a river running through northwest India, and the area that was home to one of the earliest and most advanced civilizations in the world. In fact, Hindus themselves use another name for their religion: it is *dharma* or duty. The term Hindu originally had only an ethnic meaning.

These ancient texts called the Vedas are the foundation on which Hinduism is structured. Because of their importance, it is not surprising that over the centuries commentaries were written, mainly by the brahmins or priests, and for this reason they are called the *Brahmanas,* or priestly commentaries on the Vedas. This is really not a single book but rather a whole body of literature, similar to the rabbinical commentaries on the Torah, the Talmud. These interpretations of the vedic texts became normative, and thus assumed a kind of sacred character themselves.

The final books in this category are the *Upanishads,* more commentaries, or perhaps, commentaries on the commentaries, to again cite the comparison to rabbinic literature. In these texts one finds more of the philosophical outlook of Hinduism, particularly concerning the meaning of life and the value of suffering. It is to these three groups of books that we must look to find the principal doctrines of the Hindu faith.

The next category of sacred literature is even more extensive, as it includes a large number of stories, again probably originating in an oral tradition first, which are most certainly very old, and which are filled with narratives describing the very roots of the Hindu's religious experience. The first we will mention is *The Laws of Manu,* a collection of social and religious laws first imposed on Manu, the first man, by Brahma, his creator. In this religious book the Hindu finds presented the ideals of human behavior, passed down from generation to generation. One may assume that at least parts of this book are used frequently in the religious education of the young as a kind of catechism.

Another representative text from this collection is the *Ramayana,* or story of Rama, one of the avatars of Vishnu. This long, epic poem traces the incarnation of Rama from infancy to adulthood, recounting his exploits, his teachings, and his miraculous deeds. It reads almost like one of the gospels. A similar work is the *Bhagavad Gita,* the story of Lord Krishna, another of the incarnations of Vishnu. This book constitutes the primary source of doctrine for the Krishna Consciousness Society, sometimes called the Hare Krishna sect, which is active here in the United States.

Two other works from this type of Hindu sacred literature are two collections of legends and myths. The *Mahabharata* is the story of the earliest inhabitants of the Indian Subcontinent, the Mahabharata tribe. These progenitors of the Indian race correspond with the "gods" mentioned in connection with the primitive's concept of primitive's concept of sacred time, for certainly the exploits of these people suggest a dimension which is "larger than life"—seemingly unaffected by the limitations of time and space. The final collection of stories is called just that, "ancient stories" or the *Puranas,* filled with somewhat earthy tales of warriors and heroes. As mentioned, these are not all of the books which scholars feel are part of the legacy of Hindu sacred literature, but they are probably the most popular and best known. It is from these sources that the foundations of the Hindu religion are derived.

The Caste System

Perhaps the facet of the Hindu religion best known to westerners is the caste system. Though it may be the most familiar to us, it is usually the least understood. To Americans especially the caste is something almost repugnant! When a Hindu is born into a caste, he is locked into a social, and usually economic, class from which there is no movement. This means that the "rags to riches" version of the great American dream is not possible for Hindus. Americans who live in the most mobile society on earth usually find the least mobile society on earth impossible to understand.

Westerners, in fact, will never be able to appreciate the caste system until they first come to grips with the notion of *karma*. Karma is a difficult term to define. One might call it destiny or fate, or perhaps a moral imperative. It is the belief that whatever one is in this present life is the direct result of the way one lived in his previous lifetime; and, in the same way, whatever one does in this present life will affect what one will be in a future lifetime. Obviously karma is a notion which presumes rebirth or reincarnation. One cannot understand the patient acceptance of adversity which Hindus demonstrate without first understanding their commitment to observing their karma, and karma presumes that one has lived in the past and will live again in the future. It is safe to say that in one sense heaven and hell, that is, reward and punishment, is experienced in the next lifetime.

There are four major castes. The highest caste is the *Brahmins*. This caste is sometimes called the "priestly caste," as all Hindu priests must come from this caste. In general, Brahmins are the land-owners, often wealthy, well educated, and certainly the most respected members of Indian society. The next highest caste is the *Kshatriyas,* who represent the leadership in society. In former times, Kshatriyas, have been the knights and feudal nobility in India, but today they are found in all walks of life. The chances of these being educated and assuming an important role in society are much greater than for the lower castes. The next caste is the *Vaishyas,* comprised of skilled workers, artisans, technicians, and shopkeepers. Gandhi was a member of this caste. The lowest of the four major castes is the Sudras or menial laborers. Obviously it is the largest of the castes, and poverty and illiteracy are a way of life for them.

There are two very interesting theories on how the caste system arose. They are merely theories because the caste is so old and has become such an integral part of Indian life, that no one is certain how it came into existence. One theory is called the "color theory" because it assumes that the caste was based originally on skin color. It is a fact that the Hindu word for caste is *varna*, the same word used for color. And in fact there is a noticeable gradation in skin color through the castes, with the Brahmins being for the most part much lighter than the lower castes, with the Sudras having the darkest skin color. This theory suggests that the caste system originated at the time of the Aryan invasion around 2000 B.C. It holds that the Aryans, who are of Indo-European stock, wanting to maintain the purity of their ethnic identity, instituted certain sanctions to restrict the intermarriage of its peoples with the darker, though also Caucasian, peoples of the subcontinent. This policy resulted in the stratification of Indian society into what came to be the four major castes.

The second theory draws its plausibility from the existence of hundreds and hundreds of "sub-castes." Each of these sub-castes is a division of one of the four major castes, and for the most part, each is based on some occupation. So this theory is called the "occupational theory." It suggests that early on in Indian civilization there existed hundreds of labor guilds, social and economic fraternities which eventually

A Hindu temple in Kajuraho is covered with thousands of erotic carvings, symbolic of the rich variety of religious expression in the Hindu tradition.

developed more and more rules and regulations, including the key restrictions against intermarriage and social interaction. There are in India today almost three thousand of these sub-castes.

Of course these theories are for anthropologists and historians. To the Hindu mystic the origin of the caste is quite simple. The Brahmins are the manifestations of the head and eyes of the creator, Brahma. They possess the wisdom and vision of mankind. The Kshatriyas manifest the shoulders and arms of Brahma, and thus embody his strength and power as rulers. The Vaishyas, who supply man's physical needs, represent the belly of Brahma. And the Sudras, the lowest caste, over which the others tower, are the feet of Brahma. This may be called the "mythological theory." Whichever theory may be correct, this much is known: the caste has been a tradition identified with Hinduism from time immemorial. Today in India there is evidence that some Hindus are beginning to resist some of the restrictions imposed by the caste, but it is very much a part of their lives.

One very sad and inhuman aspect of the caste is the existence of the "untouchables," or *pariahs*. Some Indians were considered outcastes, not worthy to be included in human society. They were not even to walk on the same sidewalk! This concept of untouchability is believed to have arisen possibly from the fact that leprosy was quite common in India, especially in ancient times, and these people may have been descendants of lepers. Another theory suggests that they are descendants of slaves brought to India by the Aryan conquerors, and thus were not considered freemen. Whatever its origin may have been, this perversion of human dignity was officially proscribed in the constitution of the new State of India given independence from the British Empire in 1947. Unfortunately, traditions this old die slowly.

Mohandas K. Gandhi, known to the Indian people as *Mahatma* or "great soul," worked diligently to overcome the prejudice and discrimination inherent in the caste system. He worked particularly hard to improve the status of the untouchables. Jawaharlal Nehru, a student of Gandhi's and the first prime minister of India, also opposed the caste. He once described his country as "the least tolerant nation in social forms, while the most tolerant in the realm of ideas."

"People Are Different"

It may be said that to truly appreciate Hindu religious faith one must accept the fact that Hindus do not think the same way that westerners do. In the West democracy is the ideal: everyone is equal. The Hindu way of life, in many ways, may be said to be built on the opposite belief that "people are different." With regard to the caste, for example, the proof that people are different is evidenced by the fact that everyone is born into different classes, and that fact is the direct result of the way one has lived in a previous lifetime. The circumstances into which one is born is no accident. It is either reward or punishment for one's behavior in a previous life. Part of one's karma is satisfied by the patient acceptance of one's caste. To struggle to escape the burdens of the caste is to violate one's karma, and one will surely pay the price one day. In the same way, Hindus feel no envy or bitterness at the good life enjoyed by those in the upper castes, who have each earned the privileges they possess!

There are nevertheless some redeeming features of the caste. One such positive point is the tradition that might be described with the formula, "responsibility is proportionate to privilege." By this is meant one who is privileged to be in an upper

A Hindu sadhu spends his entire life in devotion

caste is expected to be more responsible for his behavior than one in a lower caste. In fact, in the days before independence Brahmins who might commit a crime were subject to much harsher penalties than Sudras committing the same crime. Likewise, in terms of dietary restrictions and ritual laws of hygiene, Brahmins were always obliged to be more observant. It may also be argued that although society at large might be divided by the discrimination of the caste, nevertheless within each caste there was a degree of justice, security, equality, and even the opportunity to advance oneself.

Just as the concept of caste cannot be understood without penetrating the meaning of karma, neither does it make much sense apart from the Hindu's belief in reincarnation. Ultimately the whole purpose of observing one's karmic vocation in life is to reach perfection, to purify the soul or atman of all attachment to the world, and thus to prepare for the final goal of what may have been scores of lifetimes—reunion with the One, Brahman. For it is the soul which endures, the soul which journeys through many turns on the wheel of life and finally transcends all that is unreal, all that is physical and earthly. At that point the soul loses all its individuality, all its unique self-identity, and is totally absorbed into the One Reality. This is the goal of every Hindu. This acceptance of the transitory and fleeting nature of a single lifetime explains a great deal of what westerners find so perplexing in the Hindu's approach to life.

The Stages Of Life

Commitment to the belief that people are different affects not only the Hindu's resignation to the caste, but also explains his changing priorities and attitudes within a single lifetime. Hindus believe that people are different at different times in their lives, and so have different needs, goals, and means to achieve these goals. This idea explains the tradition of the stages of life.

The first stage is the Student Stage. This stage of life begins about the age of five or six, when the young Hindu boy is invested with the "sacred thread," a sign of the student stage. For the next ten or twelve years, the youngster is expected to dedicate himself to the acquisition of religious knowledge. His education in this area is supervised by a professional religious teacher called a *guru*. Gurus are highly respected by Hindus. They are not necessarily of the Brahmin caste, and therefore are not priests. The guru teaches the boys entrusted to him everything they must know to live piously, observing their karma, and practicing devotion to the gods. Due to the patriarchal nature of Hindu society, girls are not included in this experience of religious education, but are trained at home by their mothers and older sisters in the domestic arts.

The next stage is that of the Householder, and begins usually no earlier than the age of eighteen, though girls are often married at a younger age. Marriages are arranged by families which carefully select spouses for their children from families of the same caste, often of the same sub-caste. There begins now a shift in priorities. Now the Hindu is primarily concerned with providing for his family. No longer is there the leisure to spend time in devotions or *pujah* at the many shrines and temples. For twenty or thirty years or more the Hindu householder concerns himself with the material welfare of his family.

These priorities change with the next stage of life, that of Retirement. This may occur any time after the birth of the first grandchild, though financial considerations often put it off much later. In the retirement stage the Hindu begins to prepare for death, to ready his soul for the next turn of the wheel of karma. To do so the Hindu

Cows, among other animals in India, are accorded deep respect. Those past the age of usefulness
are often allowed to wander freely in the streets.

begins to disengage himself from all entanglement with the world. It is a period of gradual detachment from material things. Household items such as furniture, utensils, extra clothing—anything considered superfluous—are one by one given away, usually to the children who now have their own households for which to provide. This withdrawal from worldly attachments is considered necessary to purify the soul for its journey from this life to the next.

There is a fourth stage of life, but it is an option only some Hindu men choose. If a man's wife has predeceased him, he may decide to become a Wanderer or *sanyasi*. In effect a man becomes a monk who detaches himself completely from his family and begins to wander from shrine to shrine, to spend the remainder of his life in prayer and self-denial as a holy man. Some Hindus elect to follow the ascetical life at an early age, and so skip the middle two stages of life. Following the student stage, these young men become monks or *sadhus*. Most Hindu monks are solitaries, though there are some cenobitic orders of Hindu monks, originating, scholars believe, only after the influence of Buddhism was felt. They live celibate lives devoted to prayer and asceticism. Some of them perform remarkable and sometimes daring feats of the power of mind-over-matter. This kind of a sadhu is called a *fakir*. These holy men are found everywhere in India, especially around famous shrines where pilgrims gather. In the holy city of Benares, for example, on the banks of the River Ganges, there are liable to be ten thousand sadhus, fakirs, and sanyasi on any given day. They live simply, on the alms of the faithful who considered it both a privilege and a duty to support such selfless devotion.

The Hindu Stages Of Life

Stage	Age	Description	Goals
Student	5-6	religious education	to learn to live according to one's karma
Householder	18	married life	to provide for one's family
Retiree	after birth the birth of the first grandchild	disengagement from the material world	to prepare for the next life
Wanderer	for men whose wives are dead	complete detachment	to prepare for release from karma

The Practice Of Yoga

Another excellent example of this conviction that "people are different" is the practice of yoga which in one form or another is found universally among Hindus. Yoga is perhaps the best expression of Hindu spirituality, probably considered more important even than pujah or prayer-offerings made to the gods whether at home altars or in the many shrines and temples. Yoga comes from the Sanskrit word *yuga* which means union. The word gives us the English word, yoke, a harness or frame used to bond draft animals together as a team. The union which yoga strives to achieve is, of course, union with Brahman. One who practices yoga is called a yogi.

In recognition of the existence of different personality types, there are four principal kinds of yoga practiced by Hindus. For the person who is reflective, that is the quiet, thoughtful type, the person who enjoys solitude, there is a kind of yoga call *jnana yoga*. The technique employed in this form of yoga is basically mental prayer or meditation, perhaps contemplation. Many jnana yogis practice another type of yoga by way of preparation for jnana yoga, It is called *hatha* yoga. This is what comes to mind when most westerners see the term yoga. The object of hatha yoga is to allow one to achieve a sense of bodilessness, that is, to suppress all conscious sensation. Usually there are breathing exercises, sometimes stretching, and usually a special posture. The goal is to eliminate all distractions so that one can allow his mind to enter an undistracted, relaxed state. Many westerners find this practice an end in itself, and so hatha yoga courses are quite popular. To the real jnana yogi, however, hatha yoga is merely the preamble to meditation.

For the emotional type there is *bhakti yoga*. This type of yoga has nothing to do with meditation, but enables the yogi to achieve union with Brahman through love. Love is expressed in devotion to the gods as well as loving relationships with one's peers. This form of yoga comes close to what Christians call fraternal charity or love of neighbor. It is interesting to note that Hindus also sense the presence of God in the person of their neighbor. One can see a kind of parallel to Saint Paul's notion of the mystical "Body of Christ" in this form of Hindu spirituality.

Types Of Yoga		
Personality	**Yoga**	**Techniques**
The Reflective Person	Jnana	Mental prayer/ contemplation
The Emotional Person	Bhakti	Loving attitude toward all
The Activist Person	Karma	Charitable deeds
The Extremist Type	Rajah	Mind-over-matter exercises and out-of-body experiences
Note: Hatha Yoga exercises are especially useful to Jnana and Rajah Yogis.		

For the person who is not inclined to spend long periods in mental prayer, or who is not necessarily the emotional type, but who is what might be called an activist, one who is happiest when he or she is doing something concrete, there is *karma yoga*. The karma yogi seeks union with the godhead through the performance of good deeds. Caring for those in need, protecting the helpless, providing food and shelter to the homeless, these are the ways he chooses to seek God. The parallel with the Christian's corporal works of mercy comes to mind. The Hindus are an extremely gentle and sensitive people, and their kindness even to animals is more evidence of their awareness of God's presence throughout their earthly journey.

The River Ganges holds a special place in the Hindu religion. Here pilgrims bathe in its waters.

Although all Hindus practice some form of yoga, and many more than one, the fourth type of yoga is not for every one. Its name is *rajah yoga* which means the "royal way." This type of spirituality is embraced primarily by mystics and holy men, the fakirs mentioned earlier, for example. It appeals, one imagines, to the kind of person who is daring and willing to go to extremes in the pursuit of yogic union. In some ways like jnana yoga, involving mental concentration techniques, rajah yoga demands the development of unusual powers of psychic control and great detachment from physical limitations. The rajah yogi is determined to "leave himself" in order to attach his being to the ground of all being, Brahman, who may be found deep within himself. The union which he seeks is not so much something to be obtained or achieved but rather found, discovered within himself. Basically the method is one of divesting oneself of the illusion of individuality, escaping the sense of body, mind, and ego in order to come into contact with the true Self. Techniques vary widely, and many westerners might scoff at the sight of such a holy man's efforts. One observation that comes to mind is that in the West Sigmund Freud is often called the father of modern psychology, and yet rajah yogis have had a knowledge and appreciation of the subconscious for two thousand years.

Aum; Brahman-Atman

Hindu Sects In The West

Hinduism is what comparative religious scholars describe as an "ethnic religion," that is, one must be born a Hindu: no conversions are possible. Obviously this is due to the caste system. Nevertheless, in recent years there have been some Hindu-styled religious movements exported to the West from India.

Perhaps the best known of these is the International Society of Krishna Consciousness, frequently referred to as "the Hare Krishna Sect." With roots that lay deep in Hinduism, it is based on knowledge found in the Vedas, and is dedicated to the cult of the Lord Krishna, incarnation of Vishnu. Its goal is the achievement of pure, eternal bliss, free from all anxiety. Nothing could be more Hindu. The founder of this movement was a Hindu guru named Swami Bhaktivedanta Prabhupada. Arriving in the United States in 1965, he opened a storefront study-center in the Greenwich Village section of Manhattan, where he began to offer classes in eastern spirituality.

Meeting with only limited success in New York, Prabhupada moved to Los Angeles a short time later, establishing a similar center there. He directed his appeal primarily to young people who had become disenchanted with life, who seemed to be looking beyond the purely material world—restless, searching souls. The Swami instructed them in the ways of Hindu devotion, requiring them to live in communes called *ashrams* where they were to give themselves totally to the movement. Though no actual membership figures are ever released, today there are said to be seventy such ashrams throughout the U.S. Possibly one reason for the reluctance to reveal exact numbers is the high turn-over rate in the sect: many young people seem to be drawn by the fellowship and sense of belonging they find in the ashram, but later become disillusioned and drop out.

Members rise at 3:30 am each day for meditation and chanting. They eat a light breakfast at 7:45 and begin work at 9:15. Many go out on the streets and to public places to sell items made in the ashram by others, such as candles or incense sticks. They distribute literature about the movement and talk to whomever will listen. Frequently groups will chant the praises of the Lord Krishna publicly, accompanying themselves with drums, finger cymbals, and tambourines. Hare Krishna devotees often attract a great deal of attention, even when they are not chanting, as they all affect a Hindu style of dress and grooming. Late in the afternoon they return to the ashram where they eat a simple, vegetarian meal and retire by ten o'clock. They abstain from tea or coffee and all alchoholic beverages. The sexes are segregated, males outnumbering females usually three to one. There are some married couples and children, but even they sleep apart except for once a month.

This Hindu-styled sect has been the object of much criticism on account of its very agressive techniques of soliciting donations. Hare Krishna devotees are often accused of harassing pedestrians and obstructing traffic in public places such as airports and train stations. Another criticism has been the members of this sect seem to exhibit little genuine understanding of the movement and come across as blind adherents to their faith, something most westerners consider demeaning. In 1985 the Swami died, and the leadership of the Society was divided among a dozen or so guru- disciples. There has been a considerable amount of infighting over the succession, and accusations of mismanagement of funds, misuse of power, and the like have been exchanged by opposing factions. Recently the movement seems to be suffering from a lack of strong leadership and direction.

Another group which has experienced some success in the West is the Divine Light Mission. The original movement was founded by a famous Indian Guru known simply as the *Satguru* or "perfect master." Before he died in 1966, he passed the leadership to his third son, Sri Hans Ji Maharaj, known as Maharaj Ji, a boy in his early teens. This young guru came to the United States in 1971 to share his message, and by 1973 was able to attract almost twenty-five thousand people to a rally held in the Astrodome at Houston. Today he has over six million followers, most of whom are in India, but approximately sixty thousand live in England and the U.S.

Experience, not doctrine, is the essence of this sect. Spiritual masters called "mahatmas" instruct converts in the techniques used to obtain the special knowledge required to transcend earthly limitation and achieve bliss. Basically it is a form of meditation, dwelling on parables and paradoxes, in which the follower is encouraged to move through four stages: divine light, divine harmony, the word, and "the nectar." Somewhat like Zen, the knowledge sought is non-rational, a kind of enlightenment.

Services are punctuated with testimonies called *satsung* in which devotees share their experiences of conversion and enlightenment. Rennie Davis, who earned a reputation as a political activist during the 1960s, and in fact was indicted for his role in the demonstrations at the 1968 Democratic National Convention in Chicago, describes his conversion this way: "It gave me grace and moved me into a suppression of time and space."

Questions For Review

1. The Vedas are often described as the "sacred books" of Hinduism. How must this term be understood to distinguish them from the sacred books of Judaism, Christianity, and Islam?

2. Why is it that westerers have such difficulty in understanding the caste system?

3. Do the Hindus worship many gods or One God? Is Hinduism best described as pantheistic, polytheistic, dualistic, or monotheistic?

4. What is the concept of *karma* all about and how does it apply to the caste system?

5. How does the Hindu notion of reincarnation relate to karma and the caste system?

6. How does the expression, "People are different," seem to explain a great deal about Hindu attitudes toward life?

7. What are the stages of life for Hindus? What does this belief say about Hindu attitudes toward life?

8. Identify: karma, dharma, sadhu, fakir, sanyasi, atman, paramatman, avatar, yoga, yogi.

9. What is the practice of yoga? Why are there so many different kinds of yoga?

10. Describe the origins and basic beliefs of some of the Hindu sects that are found in North America.

In Buddhist temples the central image of the Buddha is often surrounded by those of others who, by following the Eightfold Path, have also obtained *nirvana*.

The Buddhists

The Hindu religion had been in existence for a thousand years or more when in the year 567 B.C. in north central India, not far from what is today Nepal, a son was born into the Kshatriya caste to a maharajah named Gautama—a son who would change the course of religious history in India and most of Asia. The boy's birth had been preceded by a series of visions seen by his mother and prophecies made to his father. Of course, as with many of the stories surrounding the birth and infancy of great religious figures, much of this material lies more in the realm of legend than in real history. Nevertheless, these stories have much to say about the religious significance of these figures and therefore cannot be simply dismissed as fiction.

The royal couple's visions and prophecies all pointed to a grand future for the young prince, named Siddhartha. They indicated, however, that his future would be not as a maharajah succeeding his father but as a great religious leader. This prediction was based on the great compassion with which the young prince would be blessed, a compassion that would lead him to attempt to liberate mankind from the suffering arising from old age, sickness, death, and materialism. When the child was born, however, the Maharajah determined to shield his son from the awareness of these realities. He appointed Channah, his most trusted servant, as the child's tutor and bodyguard, commanding him to exercise constant vigilance that young Siddhartha never experience these realities of life, at least until he was old enough to succeed his father.

Siddhartha's Conversion

The childhood and youthful experiences of the young prince were indeed idyllic. He grew up in the lap of luxury, securely protected from anything unpleasant. He was trained in the religious traditions of the Hindu faith, never questioning what had come to be accepted as sacred truth. At the age of eighteen he was married to the Princess Yasodarah, daughter of a neighboring maharajah. They lived happily in Gautama's palace and soon a child of their own was born, the young Prince Rahulah. Shortly thereafter, Siddhartha experienced a traumatic awakening to the seamy side of life. One day, while out for a ride in his carriage driven by the ever present Channah, Siddhartha spotted an old woman, bent over with age, along the side of the road. He or-

"...so soon as my knowledge and insight of these...noble truths...was quite purified, then was I assured what it was to be enlightened. This is my last birth. There is no more becoming for me."

—*Buddha's First Sermon*

31

dered Channah to stop the carriage, and he stepped down to question the woman, who explained her condition as simply the result of old age. Later that same afternoon, he saw a man whose body was ravaged by leprosy. Again he stopped to talk with the person to learn of his form of suffering. Still later, he observed a lifeless body lying along the side of the road. Channah was forced to explain to his royal charge the reality of death. Finally, as the story goes, the young prince caught sight of a young man, stark naked, standing in the shadows of the late afternoon transfixed in prayer. Since the young man could not or would not respond to Siddhartha's questions, Channah was forced to explain the reality of monks who fled from the entanglements of materialism to pursue a life of asceticism, total self-denial. These four encounters greatly troubled the prince. For days he could think of nothing else. He questioned Channah repeatedly about the meaning of life as presented in the holy books of Hinduism. He felt no satisfaction. Finally he made a decision which he immediately revealed to his father: he must leave the palace with its protected environment and spend whatever time was necessary to search for the key to the meaning of life.

From Prince To Monk

Siddhartha first attempted to follow the path of asceticism, denying himself even the most ordinary of physical pleasures. It is said that he subsisted during this period of his life on a single grain of rice a day. His heroic lifestyle managed to attract five other monks who found him a source of inspiration. One day, after many months of austere living, he collapsed from anemic exhaustion. Through the kindness of a stranger, he was nursed back to health, and he regained his strength. This experience taught him something: after months of this heroic exercise of ascetical discipline, he was no closer to discovering the mystery of life than before he started. He resolved to seek his goal in other ways. He began to eat normally, and even put on some additional weight.

Next, Siddhartha decided to try study. He spent many hours each day combing the Vedas for clues to the mystery confounding him: why do people suffer? Again he failed to discover the answer to his question. Almost ready to admit failure and return to the palace of his father, he decided on one last attempt. He sat down under a tree, determined to meditate for as long as it took to come to the truth. For forty-nine days and forty-nine nights he meditated, and on the morning of the fiftieth day he awoke from his trance. He had become *Buddha*, which means "the enlightened one."

He began to share his experience with any one who would listen. He now had the answers to his questions. He was able to draw several conclusions. For one thing, he realized that he had come to his enlightenment on his own: it was not through self-denial, not through knowledge of the Vedas, not even through pujah, offerings made to the gods, that he had come to this state. All these had failed him, and so he rejected them. As he shared his experience over and over again, the five monks who were first attracted to him, but later had abandoned him when he renounced the ascetical life, once again encountered the prince who had become a monk, and once again they were captivated by this man, and followed him anew. Together with them, the Buddha founded what has come to be known as the *sangha* or order of monks.

The Four Noble Truths

In the beginning, perhaps for the first two hundred years or so, the Buddha's message was a call to perfection: those who followed in his footsteps entered what was essentially the monastic state. Consequently, the Buddhist religion, if one can call it that at this point, had a very limited appeal. This explains the extremely idealistic nature of his preaching. The foundational statement of this early form of Buddhism is known as "The Four Noble Truths." In it the Buddha offered the means of liberation from an endless chain of rebirth, to which all Hindus felt themselves bound by karma.

The first truth is that life, as we experience it, is full of suffering. The word used is *dukkha*, a word which means more than physical suffering but covers all kinds of mental anguish as well. The German word, *angst*, comes close: it suggests frustration, the inability to escape failure. All human beings suffer in their lives. The second noble truth reveals that the cause of this suffering is desire, *tanha*. The word includes really three different kinds of desire: the desire for pleasure, both physical and intellectual, prosperity, or material success, and perpetuity, or continued existence. Because failure and frustration are inherent in each of these desires, we all suffer. The third truth, the Buddha concludes, is that this human suffering can be extinguished quite simply by the total eradication or uprooting of one's desires. Success in this effort enables one to experience *moksha* or release and thus to enter the state of bliss or *nirvana*. But how is one to eliminate desire, doomed as it is to bring about suffering, from one's life? This is answered in the fourth noble truth, which counsels one to follow "The Eightfold Path."

The Eightfold Path

The Eightfold Path is a collection of precepts and counsels which guide the follower on the way to enlightenment, total liberation from the bondage of the human condition. Each of the paths—not understood as sequential steps, but rather as congruent techniques used by the follower to achieve his goal of perfection—each are qualified by the term "right." This is to be interpreted as representing the Buddha's counsel of moderation, that is the avoidance of the extremes of excess and defect both: neither trying too hard nor too little. The precondition of the paths is something called "right association." By this is meant that one should seek the company of others inclined to the same pursuit of perfection. In this way one will be inspired and encouraged by the example of others struggling toward the same objective. In simple terms, this seems to mean that one should enter the sangha if one is serious about perfection. Only in this rarified atmosphere of the monastic lifestyle can one be successful in eluding the allurements of the world or *maya*, from which all desires come.

The first of the paths is right understanding. This means that one must, above all, affirm the validity of the Four Noble Truths. It is only with this conviction that one can begin to make progress. Right mindedness or right intention concerns one's commitment to the goal of liberation. Right speech is the admonition to speak little, and then always in truth and charity. The fourth of the paths is called right action. It mandates excluding from one's life certain harmful deeds: do not kill, do not steal, do not lie, do not be unchaste, and do not drink intoxicating beverages. In general this path requires one to avoid any self-seeking or unkind actions. It may be regarded as the Buddhist

The Buddha is frequently depicted with elongated ears, a symbol of his receptivity to enlightenment.

version of the Ten Commandments. Right living has to do with one's employment. No one may have a job which takes life rather than promotes it: work must be productive, not destructive. Right effort has to do with the pace of one's spiritual progress. Avoid binges: make slow but steady progress, avoiding the start-and-stop approach to the spiritual life. Right attentiveness involves a constant evaluation of one's motives and desires, and is much like the examination of conscience with which Christians are so familiar. The final path, that of right concentration, is perhaps the clearest indication of the monastic orientation to early Buddhism, for it requires one to hold the goal of perfection as one's principal focus in life, something not always possible for those in the lay state.

For many years the Buddha and his monk-disciples moved about India, preaching the message of liberation through enlightenment and attracting additional converts. So committed to the concept of detachment, they did not even have a permanent dwelling. They soon earned the somewhat derogatory nickname of "tree-dwellers" because they often slept in trees. There is a legend that describes the Buddha returning to his home after many years absence and revealing himself to his father and wife and son, who hardly recognized him. The legend has Yasodarah begging her husband to allow her to follow his path to enlightenment herself, and Siddhartha directing her to found a sangha for women. Scholars, however, believe that the existence of Buddhist nuns originated much later, perhaps centuries.

The Buddhist Scriptures

The Buddha died at the age of eighty, surrounded by his monks. In order to preserve the teachings of their master, the monks began to put to writing some of his ideas. This effort culminated in the scriptures called the *Tipitaka* or "baskets of truth." The first of these is the *Sutta Pitaka* which contains the sayings of the Buddha. Like so many other disciples of religious leaders, they sought to preserve for all time the wisdom of the master. The second part of this collection of sacred writings is the *Vinaya Pitaka,* which sets down the rules of the sangha, establishing the lifestyle that Buddhist monks observe even today all over Asia. In addition to the five precepts already mentioned as part of the path of right conduct, the monks observe five other commandments: not to take solid food after midday, not to sing or dance or attend the theater, not to wear jewelry, use perfumes, or dress extravagantly, not to sleep on comfortable beds, and not to accept monetary gifts. These regulations may be found in the Vinaya. The third part is the *Abhidhamma Pitaka,* by far the longest of these texts, which is a collection of commentaries, in many ways more philosophical than religious.

When he died in the year 487 B.C., the Buddha's disciples may have numbered in the hundreds, but certainly not many more than that. It is quite probable that they were regarded simply as one more of the many sects within Hinduism, and not as a new religion. This new sect might have been considered in some ways a reform movement within Hinduism because of its fresh approach to old concepts. Because the Buddha rejected so many of the traditional ideas of the Hindu faith, however, one might well question its being considered a religion at all.

Was Early Buddhism A Religion?

This question is indeed a legitimate one because all of the world's religions seem to share at least to some degree six elements in common: authority, tradition, ritual, speculation, grace, and mystery. By authority is meant the structured organization of a religion. Early Buddhism, aside from the monastic disciplines set down in the Vinaya Pitaka, which may in fact have come into existence much later, appears to have none of this. The monks, like so many of their contemporaries among Hindu ascetics, lived somewhat independently. There appears to be little evidence of the exercise of binding authority.

By tradition is meant the transmission of thought and understanding from one generation to the next, that is, some form of normative interpretation of the meaning of key concepts and doctrines. The Buddha adamantly opposed such strictures, and before he died ordered his followers to burn all of his writings and to preserve nothing of what he taught. They were to seek enlightenment on their own, and without any outside direction. Fortunately, those disciples decided to ignore his request. Nevertheless, there remained a very individualistic approach to perfection, with a great deal of variation tolerated.

By ritual is meant any kind of prayers or offerings made to the gods. As has been noted already, Siddhartha rejected this. He did not deny the existence of the gods; he merely saw no use in supplications made to them. Each person achieved nirvana through his own efforts.

Not all religions possess the element of speculation, which may be defined as the means by which knowledge of the sacred is achieved through the use of human reason. One might equate this element with the western religious concept of theology. Siddhartha had rejected the value of the Vedas and taught that enlightenment was something that need only be discovered within oneself.

Grace may be defined as the relationship one enjoys with the sacred, the bond that unites an individual with the godhead. The Hindu may have seen this relationship expressed in his karmic vocation, that is, his responsiblity to live out his lifetime in the caste in which he was born. The Buddha clearly rejected the caste, as he taught that anyone, no matter what caste, might achieve enlightenment in a single lifetime.

"Is Buddhism A Religion At All?
Key Elements In Any Religion

Element	Christianity	Hinduism	Classic Buddhism
Authority	Pope & Bishops	Brahmins	
Tradition	Tradition	Sacred Books	
Ritual	Sacraments	Pujah	
Speculation	Theology	Brahmanas	
Grace	Grace	Karma	
Mystery	Eucharist	Yoga	

By mystery is meant the possibility of participating in the sacred order of being, that is, the escape from the limitations of time and space incumbent on the human condition. One thinks of the Hindu practice of yoga. No such temporary release from the human condition was considered possible in early Buddhism. Nirvana, once achieved, was permanent and final.

What then was the earliest form of Buddhism if not a religion? One might regard it as a self-improvement program, a system of ethics, or perhaps a philosophy of life, but hardly a religion since it appears to have had none of the hallmarks of traditional religion.

Two Great Traditions

But what about today? Isn't Buddhism considered a legitimate religion today? It is, of course. The reason for the change in status is that over the years the moral philosophy endorsed by Siddhartha Gautama has evolved: it has developed into a religion. Today there are two great traditions within Buddhism, and that division and how it occurred is the key to Buddhism becoming a religion. For at least two centuries Buddhism remained a little known and little accepted sect within the great Hindu tradition of holy men, appealing mostly to a select few who were willing to embrace the monastic state in order to follow the path of the Buddha to enlightenment.

In the middle of the Third Century B.C. an ambitious maharajah named Asoka began to dream of empire. One by one he was able to conquer the armies of neighboring states, until soon he ruled almost a third of the sub-continent. To unify his new empire, so divided by dialect and caste, he decided to impose upon his new subjects a new religion. He himself had been impressed by the teachings of the Buddha and considered this man the equal of any avatar of the gods. In order to make this new faith acceptable to the masses, Asoka decreed that certain adaptations be made in the Buddhist tradition.

Now those monks who followed the Buddha's teachings, as they were originally presented, did exactly what one would expect: they resisted what they considered to be an adulteration of their faith. This resistance to change and innovation gave rise to what are known today as the two main traditions of Buddhism. The new version was called *mahayana,* or the wide road to perfection, and the original version which the monks struggled to preserve from corruption was called *hinayana,* or the narrow road. The monks preferred to call their interpretation *theravada,* or the religion of the elders. In time both not only survived but prospered, each continuing to evolve.

Some of the differences between Mahayana and Hinayana Buddhism are glaring; others are more subtle. Obviously there is a strong monastic bent to Theravada Buddhism. All males enter the monastery for at least a part of their lives, even if only for a month or two. Many enter the monastery as youngsters and receive their education with the monks. Whenever they do so, whether as children or adults, they actually become monks, shaving their heads, taking the monk's simple robe, participating in the common prayer and chanting from the Tipitaka, and submitting themselves completely to the elder monks. In Mahayana only some males enter the monastery. There is no feeling of compulsion, as the laity also are respected as authentic disciples of the Buddha's path to enlightenment. There is in Hinayana a definite individualistic approach: each person is responsible for his own salvation, whereas in Mahayana there is more of a community spirit, that is, one feels the responsibility to assist his neighbor in

Empire of Asoka, 250 B.C.E.

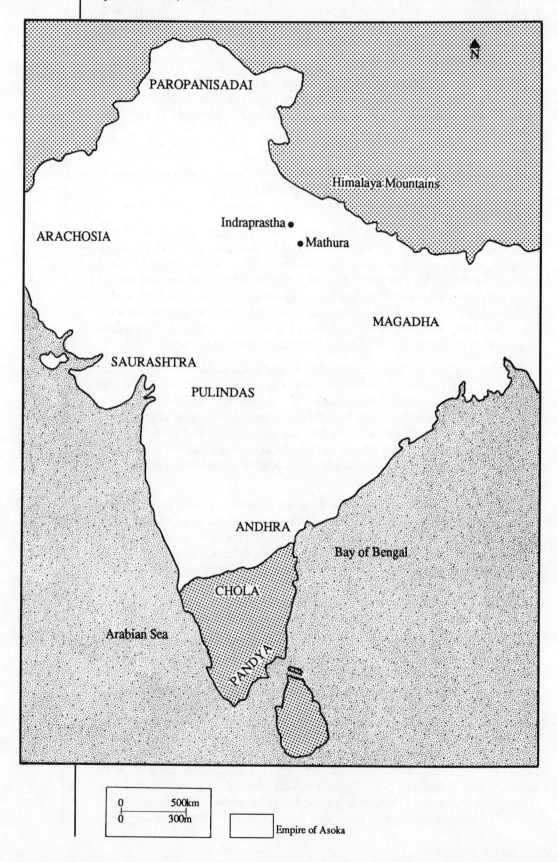

achieving enlightenment. Instead of the solitary meditation characteristic of Hinayana, there is an emphasis on prayer and offerings in Mahayana. This points to what is probably the most striking difference in the two traditions. For Hinayana or Theravada Buddhism, the Buddha is a great teacher, a visionary, a guide to perfection, but just a man, a human being who had entered the state of eternal bliss. With Mahayana Buddhism the Buddha is considered more than just a man: he was a human being who has so transcended earthly limitations that he has become divine. And so, with Mahayana Buddhism the Buddha is worshipped. He is the recipient not only of honor and respect, but also of prayer and offerings—pujah.

Buddhism Spreads

One might expect that Buddhism would then have become a major religion in India, rivaling in popularity even the timeless Hinduism. This was not to be the case. By the year 1000 A.D., Islam had spread into India, hand in hand with the expansion of the Second Arab Empire. The Mogul rulers were generally intolerant of the "infidels," and persecutions abounded. Buddhist monks resisted, and, rather than remain in India and fight for their religious freedom, they began to emigrate to other parts of Asia. This historical turning-point in Indian history became the impetus for a massive missionary movement of Buddhism to other nations. This migration had already begun on a somewhat lesser scale two or three centuries earlier, but now the exodus from India began in earnest. Unlike Hinduism, Buddhism was unencumbered by the restriction of the caste, and so the Buddhist faith could be embraced by anyone. It was not ethnic but universalist in its orientation.

Mahayana monks moved in the direction of central and northern Asia, while Hinayana missionaries seemed to concentrate on southern Asia. Today, of the world's three or four hundred million Buddhists, the vast majority are found outside India where the religion originated. The countries of Tibet, China, Mongolia, Korea, and Japan have adopted the mahayana faith, while Sri Lanka (Ceylon), Burma, Thailand, Cambodia, Laos, and Viet Nam follow the hinanyana tradition. One can notice immediately one of the major distinctions in the two traditions when visiting these countries, for in those of central and northern Asia where Mahayana Buddhism is popular you see enormous statues of the god-like Buddha, sometimes several stories tall, whereas in hinayana countries such larger-than-life representations of the Buddha are rare. Likewise, in hinayana areas the monks are quite numerous, and sometimes wield considerable power and influence among the people, as was witnessed in Viet Nam.

Distinctive Features Of	
Hinayana Buddhism	**Mahayana Buddhism**
Individualistic	Group-Oriented
Follower creates own destiny	One gets help from others
Very monastic in attitude	Less monastic
Meditation on Self	Prayer to others for assistance
Follower seeks own good	Follower must help others
Buddha is Leader, Guide	Buddha is more like God
Popular is Southern Asia	Popular in Central and Northern Asia

One feature of Mahayana Buddhism which expedited its spread into other countries appears to have been the mahayana concept of the *bodhisattva*. This is the belief that one who has achieved enlightenment, and who therefore has become another buddha or enlightened one, may defer entrance into nirvana or the state of bliss in order to assist others to reach the same goal. These heroic souls then become models and itercessors for those still struggling for moksha or release from the bondage of maya. In the mahayana view they are like the gods of other religions—to be praised and supplicated. Armed with this belief, mahayana missionary monks could thus permit other peoples to retain their own gods, as long as they understood them to be "bodhisattvas." In other words, one did not have to renounce his own religion completely to embrace Buddhism. This feature accounts for the mixed character of Mahayana Buddhism: how it seems to blend with rather than usurp native religions in the countries to which it spread.

Buddhism And Christianity

One might wonder how Buddhism ought to be designated as a religion: is it pantheistic, polytheistic, dualistic, or monotheistic? In order to answer this question, one must first determine which tradition of Buddhism one is talking about. The easier of the two main traditions to classify would, of course, be mahayana. With its openness to the beliefs already found in the countries to which it spread, together with the place given to the bodhisattvas, one would have to say that Mahayana Buddhism is best described as polytheistic. On the other hand, with its agnostic approach to the gods, together with its emphasis on finding perfection within oneself, Hinayana Buddhism may best be considered part of the pantheistic family of religions. One should recall, however, that these categories may mean more to westerners than to others. Some Buddhists may argue that the uniqueness of their faith defies categorization.

It is nevertheless interesting to compare religions around the world, and Buddhism is no exception. For example, there are a number of similarities between Buddhism and Christianity. Both religions are offshoots of older, more established parent religions. In addition, they each were considered from the beginning something of reform movements, at first simply a sect within the parent religion, albeit one which had some major differences with the mainstream, and only some time later actually separated. Both Buddhism and Christianity, unlike their parent faiths had historical founders—real people who were born into the parent faith, and then founded a religious movement. Curiously, both Siddhartha and Jesus were proclaimed divine only after their deaths.

Ironically, both Buddhism and Christianity seemed to expand and flourish only when they moved outside the land of their origin. This fact suggests still another similarity: both religions have a strong missionary character, based on a universalist orientation as well as a desire to spread the "good news" of the possibility of liberation from the bondage of the human spirit. Both place strong emphasis on the pursuit of perfection, and for this reason have a long tradition of monasticism. The vision of the afterlife in Buddhism, with its reward of eternal bliss for the soul who has been truly liberated from bondage to this world, certainly has more in common with Christianity than with Hinduism. Finally, the concept of the bodhisattvas found in mahayana seems to approach the Christian idea of the saints, those who have demonstrated heroic virtue in their lives and are thus held up for veneration.

Zen Buddhism

Perhaps the best known form of Buddhism in the West is Zen. Althought this variation was developed in Japan, its origins can be traced back through China to India. About a thousand years after the death of Siddhartha, in the Sixth Century A.D., an Indian monk of the mahayana tradition named Bodhidharma came to realize that the mahayana form of Buddhism had lost something valuable which the hinayana form had always retained, namely the individualistic nature of salvation with an emphasis on solitary meditation as the source of enlightenment. He started to share his ideas on the techniques of mental power with his fellow monks. This development was soon known as *dyhana*. It so happened that Bodhidharma was one of the Buddhist monks who journeyed to China to spread the faith. He took Dyhana Buddhism with him.

There in China Dyhana Buddhism received the Chinese name of cha'an, which translates literally as "sitting." During the course of the next two or three centuries, the followers of this form of Buddhism divided over the issue of how enlightenment occurs. Some argued that it comes instantaneously in the same manner that Siddhartha himself had come to this blessed state. Others felt that such was not ordinarily the case, but rather for most enlightenment was the end result of a long process, one which might in fact take a lifetime. These factions split in two different schools of Cha'an Buddhism.

Beginning in the Ninth Century, Buddhism began to move into Japan. At this time Chinese merchants and explorers were staging a kind of invasion of Japan, taking along with them many of the elements of Chinese culture, including religion and philosophy. Compared to the highly developed culture and economy of the Chinese, the Japanese were still in the dark ages so to speak, and so were quite open to the far reaching influences of Chinese culture. In Japan dyhana, now cha'an, became *za-zen*.

The two schools of cha'an assumed new names too. The form of cha'an which envisioned instantaneous enlightenment was called *rinzai,* and that which promoted the idea of enlightenment as process was called *soto*. These two schools of Buddhism have endured down through history into the modern era. There have been other variations, but these two remain the most important. As so often happened with the mahayana tradition of Buddhism, there occurred over the years some absorption of foreign concepts which gradually became part of the original. In this case cha'an, which had been subject to the influence of Taoism in China, assumed a somewhat new dimension with a keen interest in nature. This aspect of cha'an found a welcome place with the Japanese who had always revered nature as a sacred force. In summary, Zen Buddhism, so popular in Japan and even in the West today, is the result of a fusion of elements derived from Buddhism and Taoism.

This enlightenment which is the goal of Zen is called *satori*. This knowledge is not acquired through the senses, as other kinds of knowledge, but rather is already within each person, a kind of innate or inborn knowledge which need only be discovered through meditation. Satori therefore is simply discovery. Often one meditates on a paradoxical statement or a riddle with the hope of making the breakthrough. One of the most famous of these riddles or *koans* is "the sound of one hand clapping."

It should perhaps be noted here that, due to the amorphous nature of Zen Buddhism, the techniques of Zen are often practiced by those who are not Buddhists in order to achieve a kind of inner peace and sense of well-being. The methods of Zen meditation, for example, are often used to increase one's ability to concentrate and perform tasks

A Buddhist monk in Thailand, dressed in the traditional monk's robe, and with shoes removed, prays with other Buddhists.

more efficiently. Even athletes have been known to meditate before important competitions. It is also interesting to note that the Trappist monk, Thomas Merton, died while on a lengthy visit to Japan where he was studying the principles of Zen meditation with the hope of adapting them for his own contemplative community in Gethsemane, Kentucky.

Buddhism In Tibet

A unique expression of buddhism may be found in Tibet. This type of Buddhism is often referred to as Lamaism, after the Tibetan word for monk which is *lama,* or sometimes Tantric Buddhism, which is a variation of mahayana often associated with a complex form of a ritualism with roots in the Hindu cult of Shiva and his consort, Durga. Perhaps the most interesting aspect of Tibetan Buddhism is the history of its monks actually ruling the country as a veritable theocracy.

Buddhism first arrived in Tibet in the Seventh Century when a king married a princess from Nepal just across the Himalayan Mountains. This princess brought her religion with her, as a number of monks accompanied her to her new homeland. Gradually, these monks began to make some converts among the Tibetans and built the first Buddhist monastery. In the following century another king married, this time a Chinese princess, also a Buddhist, who also brought with her a group of monks who also built monasteries. Soon Tibetans were converting to this new religion in large numbers. There were two sects of monks, originating from two different countries, but sharing the mahayana tradition of Buddhism.

By the Ninth Century Buddhism had become the state religion, established and supported by the rulers. Heavily mixed with elements of the native religion, which was basically animistic, this form of Buddhism became a somewhat distant cousin of the original version founded by Gautama. It was filled with rituals, incantations, and mystical symbolism unknown to more traditional forms of the religion. Richly endowed monasteries were everywhere; the monks grew comfortable and lax. Some even married. Monasteries became secular institutions—centers of education, politics, and commerce. At times during this period as many as one-fifth of the male inhabitants of Tibet were monks, at least of a sort. This was the sad state of Buddhism at the beginning of the Eleventh Century when the Mongolian Empire under its powerful ruler, the Altan Khan, began to expand. With the Mongols at the gates as it were, factions began to divide the Tibetan people. The monks who traced their roots back to China, and who were known as "the Yellow Sect," decided that prudence was the better part of valor and the best policy to take was that of collaboration. The Mongols were going to conquer the country anyway, so why not welcome them and save a lot of bloodshed. The monks who traced their roots back to India, and who were called "the Red Sect" (both names, incidentally, are derived from the color of the hats the monks wore), opted for the policy of resistance.

In the end, the Mongols did in fact easily conquer the country, and it did not take the Khan long to determine who his friends were. Not wishing to delay his plans for the continued expansion of his empire through conquest, he named the head monk of the Yellow Sect as his proxy ruler, bestowing on him the title *Dalai,* which translates "holder of the thunderbolt." By this act the Dalai Lama became the virtual ruler of Tibet. For many centuries the Dalai Lama exercised complete control both politically and religiously over his people, thus ruling what amounted to a theocracy, where both spheres of authority are joined in one office. During part of this time, the Dalai Lama was ordinarily succeeded by his own son. He lived in a large "monastery" defended by "monk-soldiers." By the Fifteenth Century, with the decline of the Mongol Empire, Tibet had become virtually independent, but retained the same governmental structure with its "monk-king." Later in this same century a remarkable reform of the monasteries was undertaken, with the discipline of celibacy restored.

By far the most interesting thing to westerners about Tibetan Lamaism has to be the manner of choosing the successor to a deceased Dalai Lama. The method is tied to the belief that the Dalai Lama is a reincarnation of the Buddha himself. When he died, a search was conducted throughout the country to determine which male infant was born closest to the moment of his death. Usually several possible successors were identified and then brought to the main monastery at Lhasa Apso, the capitol. The parents of these infants would be honored that their own sons might be the reincarnation of the deceased Dalai Lama, and so gladly turned them over to the monks. The boys would be raised at the monastery until a series of investigations and scrutinies could be undertaken. The youngsters might be asked to identify certain personal objects used by the Dalai Lama among others with no connection to him whatsoever. Those who failed to do so would gradually be eliminated from consideration and sent home, until just one candidate survived the tests. He then would be proclaimed the actual manifestation, to be educated by the senior monks until the day he could be crowned. The present Dalai Lama, the fourteenth, was born in 1935 and identified in just this manner in 1937. Enthroned in 1940, he ruled Tibet until the invasion by Communist China and its immediate annexation to the People's Republic of China in 1950. He fled to neighboring India in 1959 and now lives in exile in New Delhi, awaiting the day he can be restored to his people.

Questions For Review

1. How would you describe the "conversion" of Siddhartha Gautama?

2. Explain what is meant by the Four Noble Truths and the Eightfold Path.

3. Was the classic concept of Buddhism as preached by the Buddha and his early followers really a religion as we understand religion today? Explain.

4. The earliest form of Buddhism might be described as a "call to perfection." Explain.

5. What comparisons can be drawn between Buddhism and Christianity?

6. What significant, historical development occurred which transformed Buddhism from what was basically a variant form of Indian monasticism into a religion embraced by millions all across Asia?

7. Contrast the principal differences between the two great traditions of Buddhism in the world today.

8. Define the term, "reform." Using this definition, describe the ways that Buddhism can be seen as a reform of the Hindu religion.

9. Trace the origins of that sect of Buddhism called "Zen." What is the single goal of all Zen Buddhists, and what techniques do they use to achieve it?

10. What is meant by the term, "Tantric Buddhism?" Where is this form of Buddhism most prevalent? What is so unique about it?

11. Identify: dukkha, tanha, moksha, nirvana, maya, Tipitaka, King Asoka, Mahayana, bodhisattva, Hinayana, Theravada, sangha, Bodhidharma, soto, rinzai, dhyana, cha'an, za-zen, Dalai Lama.

This temple in Calcutta, built as a tribute to the Tirthankaras, is a good example of the very elaborate and beautiful architecture of Jain temples.

The Jains

The Jains represent only a tiny fraction of the population of India. Out of almost three-quarters of a billion inhabitants of the sub-continent, only about two or three million are Jains. This religion does not interest us because of its numerical significance. Rather it is the uniqueness of the expressions of its religious beliefs which captivates us. Foremost among these expressions is the practice of total non-violence or ahimsa. Many of the world's great religions hold non-violence as an ideal, but none observe this ideal as perfectly as the Jains. It is indeed unique.

The existence of the Jain religion adds fuel to the argument that in its earliest form Buddhism was considered simply another sect within the Hindu tradition, for the Jain religion may have begun in the same manner. There are certainly many similarities. Its founder was an Indian of the Kshatriya caste, named Vardhamana, the son of a maharajah, born in the Sixth Century, B.C., who left his life of ease and comfort to seek the ultimate meaning of life. The parallel with the story of Siddhartha should be obvious. Beyond a few details, probably more legend than fact, little is known about this man.

Actually there are three theories on the origin of Jainism. The first theory suggests that Vardhamana was in fact a real person who, like Siddhartha, founded a religion which was also a kind of reform of Hinduism. Some of his ideas were similar to Buddhism, but others were closer to the parent faith. A second theory has Jainism being another of the many factions within the Hindu religious tradition, which years, perhaps centuries later, in imitation of the Buddhists, then mythologized the existence of a real human founder. Hence the many similarities between the two founders. Still a third theory would have the Jains breaking away from the Buddhists, and then mythologizing a separate founder to accentuate its uniqueness. The existence of the second and third theories is based on the assumption that since so little is known about the founder of the Jains, it is unlikely that he ever lived.

"This is the quintessence of wisdom: not to kill anything. Know this to be the legitimate conclusion from the principle of reciprocity..."

—*Commentary on the Angas*

The Story Of Vardhamana

The story of Vardhamana is extremely close to that of Siddhartha. He was born in the same century, in approximately the same part of India, also the son of a maharajah, though not the eldest but the second son. It is said that before his birth his mother had fourteen dreams predicting that her son would be a great leader of the people, though not as a secular leader but as a religious one. In his childhood Vardhamana was given a special nickname by his playmates. One afternoon, while they were playing together outside the palace, a spooked elephant came charging across the lawn. The children scattered for safety, all except Vardhamana who stood his ground. As the elephant charged past, young Vardhamana hoisted himself atop the elephant and, calming him, rode him back to the stables. When he rejoined his playmates, they all cried out, "Mahavira! Mahavira!" The name, meaning "great hero," stuck. Thenceforth he was known as Mahavira to his friends. A portent of the future?

When Vardhamana was eighteen he experienced a real trauma in his life. His parents who were devout Hindus, seeing that their eldest son was now of age and able to assume his father's throne, decided to end their lives and prepare to enter the next cycle of birth, hopefully as Brahmins. They locked themselves in their chambers and, refusing to eat or drink, slowly starved themselves to death. This custom was acceptable to the Hindu tradition, but Vardhamana could not accept it. For days and nights he pondered the meaning of life, but remained unable to understand why his parents had ended their lives in their prime years. He sought his older brother's permission to leave the palace, and to spend whatever time was necessary to discover this mystery which eluded him. His brother, now crowned the new maharajah, refused his younger brother's wish, and counselled patience. He insisted that it would be unfair for the younger children to lose their older brother as well as their parents at the same time. And so Vardhamana waited. He studied the Vedas, searching them for the wisdom he needed to understand his parents' act. He found no answer to his question. It is believed that during this time he entered into a marriage arranged for him by his older brother, but still he found no escape from the burden of his great sorrow. Finally, the day came when his brother gave in to his petitions and allowed Vardhamana to leave the palace and become a wanderer.

Embracing the life of an ascetic, Vardhamana wandered about India from shrine to shrine. So impressive was the holiness of his lifestyle that other monks followed him. It is assumed that he somehow found peace in his life with the monks. Nevertheless, no such dramatic statements as one sees in the Four Noble Truths of Buddhism survived him. The sangha continued after his death and perpetuated the memory of this man. After his death, many of his sayings were recorded in a book called the *Angas* or *Agamas*. This is all that is known about him. One can appreciate why there are different theories about the origins of this religion. The parallels are so close to those of Buddhism, one is quite justified in assuming that he may never have lived, but is rather the creation of myth-makers.

The Tirthankaras

The place of Mahavira, as he is now exclusively called in the Jain religion, is likewise similar to that of Siddhartha. He is considered to be divine, or to have become divine. One might ask then why the religion is not called "Mahavirism." The answer to this question throws further light on the nature of Jainism. The name Jain is derived from the Indian word *jina* which means "conqueror." Jains believe that the ultimate duty of every person is to conquer the evil within oneself. Each soul contains both good and evil, *jiva* and *ajiva*. Those who are able to eliminate all the ajiva within themselves are conquerors or "jinas." They believe that there have been forty-eight such perfect conquerors, twenty-four who lived in pre-history and twenty-four who lived in history. Mahavira is acknowledged as the last conqueror or *tirthankara* in the second cycle. He has become divine, but he is not alone. Nor are these tirthankaras divine in the same sense we in the West might use the word. In fact they are probably closer to the "divinity" of the bodhisattvras in Buddism. They are heroes and models of human behavior. Jains honor these jinas, and aspire to imitate them. The temples and shrines erected in their honor are more like the memorials we build to our heroes and leaders than they are to our churches and synagogues.

Non-Violence And The Jains

The Jains are certainly an ascetical people. They practice detachment from worldly pleasures and sensitivity to other living beings to a remarkable degree. In fact their non-violence or *ahimsa* is the very hallmark of their religious commitment. Jains believe that it is evil to take the life of any living being. For this reason Jains take what most would consider extraordinary precautions to avoid taking life. The notion of ahimsa is found in the Eightfold Path of Buddhism as well. In the Fourth Path, that of right conduct, is found the prohibition agianst killing. Jains simply take this to the extreme. Jains are, for example, like Buddhists, vegetarians, but no Jain, may even harvest the fruits or vegetables he eats, seeing that as an act of violence against the plant; nor may he cook them, for in that act of boiling water tiny microscopic beings are killed. How then do they eat? Jains are found only among the upper classes of Indian society, and therefore can afford to have servants prepare their meals. Jains, unlike the Buddhists, have not abandoned the caste altogether. They maintain a different kind of caste system, not social but spiritual. They believe that taking life under any circumstances whatsoever is evil for them, but not so for their non-Jain servants, who are living on a lesser plane and who consequently have lesser responsibilities.

Jains are equally sensitive to insect life. Few go outdoors during the rainy season as so many living creatures are washed down out of the trees during the heavy rains so common in India. Even during the dry season, most Jains carry "sweepers," made usually of fallen peacock feathers to sweep away any living creatures beneath their feet as they walk. Some Jains even wear masks covering their mouths and nostrils to prevent the inadvertent swallowing or inhalation of flying insects. Jain monks consider it a daily duty to go through their meager belongings with a duster to remove gently any living beings there. This remarkable sensitivity to the value of life even on lower levels is exemplified further by the custom of wealthy Jains building and maintaining pet hospitals whose charge is the healing of wounded birds and animals which are found and brought to the care of these institutions.

There are two main sects among the Jainist monks: the Swetembara sect or "white clad" monks, and the Digembara or "sky-clad" monks. This latter group do not even wear white robes as their Swetembara counterparts do, but they are nudists, feeling even the possession of a simple robe is an attachment to material things. Both of these sanghas are highly respected by all Jains, who see it as their duty to support the monks in their commitment to the ascetical life. Monks have little to do with the laity, not even officiating at rituals such as marriage or funerals. They are expected to devote themselves totally to the spiritual life. So important is monasticism to the essence of Jainism, there is even a sangha for nuns. Here is seen one more similarity with the Buddhists, though which religion first offered the monastic option to women is not certain.

A Comparison

It is interesting to note the number of concepts and customs found in Jainism which reflect Buddhist influence and which reflect that of Hinduism. One very close parallel to Hinduism is the Jainist custom of marking three different stages of life. They are simply called the prime, the middle, and the final stages. Like Hindus, Jains have a student stage into which young Jain boys are inducted with a special ceremony featuring the taking of twelve vows. The vows themselves suggest the influence of the monastic life on the laity. The vows are solemn promises made to keep the moral precepts of the religion. The middle stage is that of the householder, married life. Again this stage is marked by the taking of vows, eleven in number—the vow of sexual abstinence is the one dropped. The third stage is that of retirement and preparation for death and rebirth, again reflecting the Hindu stage. To inaugurate this stage of life, five vows are taken, much like the vows by which the monks themselves are bound. During this final stage, it is not unusual for very wealthy Jains to distribute everything they own, to emphasize their detachment from material things, in order to prepare for their next life.

Jainism Is Like:	
Hinduism	**Buddhism**
It has a "kind of a caste" (moral rather than social)	It rejects polytheism
Observes non-violence to a remarkable degree	Detachment from the world
Very ascetical in nature	Has organized system of monasticism
Observes "stages of life"	The Jinas are like the Bodhisattvas

There are a number of other concepts and customs which reflect the influences of these other Indian religions. The spiritual caste system which the Jains have adopted, considering themselves above others and therefore bound by higher laws, certainly suggests a strong Hindu influence. On the other hand, the veneration with which the jinas or tirthankaras are honored seems to indicate the influence of the Buddhist notion of the bodhisattvas. In many ways the Jainist idea of the relationship between the individual and ajiva suggests the Buddhist approach to worldly temptations called maya. The ideal of asceticism, rejected by the Buddha, and by Buddhist monks, as unnecessary and unproductive, is embraced wholeheartedly by Jains, especially by the monks, again belying a strong Hindu influence. The Jainist idea of the after-life, however, is certainly closer to Buddhism than Hinduism. Jains believe in an individualized existence in the after-life, with a rather well developed version of reward and punishment: there are twenty-six levels of heaven and seven levels of hell for Jains. Even the Jain scriptures, the Angas, which include a collection of sayings of the founder, remind one of the Sutta Pitaka. In addition there are commentaries on the Angas, called the Upangas, which may be compared with other parts of the Tipitaka. Lastly, the existence of the great sanghas of monks and nuns, with an elaborate system of rules and regulations, and especially the option of community living, demonstrates the influence of Buddhist monasticism.

Another Form Of Pantheism?

Despite the appearance of polytheism evident in the devotion which Jains have for their Tirthankaras, Jainism is basically another form of pantheism. Because it has necessarily remained small, and has not expanded into other countries as has Buddhism, it has not been mixed up with the worship of other deities, as has Mahayana Buddhism especially. And certainly the reverence for life in all its forms, even the very lowest, suggests the firm belief in the sacredness of all of creation.

Questions For Review

1. Give three different theories as to the origin of the Jain religion.

2. Which features of Jainism are closer to the Hindu religion, and which features are closer to the Buddhist tradition?

3. Why is the Indian religious concept of *ahimsa* considered the essence and soul of Jainism? Cite some examples of how this belief is expressed in Jain life.

4. Write an essay entitled, "A Jain Comes to Visit," in which you imagine a Jain coming to the United States and reacting to the violence of everyday life here. The essay may be subtitled, "A Look at a Violent Culture through Non-Violent Eyes."

5. Identify: Vardhamana, Mahavira, Angas, Upangas, ahimsa, Digembara, Swetembara, sweepers, jiva, ajiva, jinas, tirthankaras.

Three generations of Sikhs, dressed according to the Law of Khalsa.

The Sikhs

From the three Indian religions which originated in the time before Christ, we now turn our attention to a more "modern" religion which originated at the end of the Fifteenth Century. The Sikh religion, like Jainism, is more of interest to us because of its uniqueness than because of sheer numbers. Today Sikhs are to be found all over the world, and yet more than half of the fifteen or sixteen million of them are concentrated in one small section of India called the Punjab, located in northwest India. This of course represents only about two percent of the total population of the sub-continent, and yet this religious minority has exerted a great influence on modern India.

A Hybrid Religion

The uniqueness of the Sikh faith lies primarily in the manner in which it was conceived and brought into being. It represents a kind of hybrid or mixture of two major world religions which were in existence in India at the time of its foundation: elements were drawn from Hinduism and Islam to form a compromise between the two faiths. This process of combining different elements from two or more religious traditions to form a new religion is called "syncretism." Comparative religion scholars frequently distinguish two types of syncretism, conscious and unconscious. By conscious syncretism, is meant the deliberate choice of religious ideas to fabricate a new religion; by unconscious syncretism is meant the more or less accidental, and certainly more gradual, absorption of religious ideas from different religions which coexist in the same area. Sikhism is a prime example of conscious syncretism because its founder deliberately set about establishing a new religion which would be a compromise.

India in the Fifteenth Century was a land in religious turmoil. Beginning around the year 1000, the Moslems had invaded and conquered most of northwest India. It was this invasion which signaled the demise of Buddhism in India, so that today fewer than ten million Buddhists are left there. As the Second Arab Empire expanded, its mogul rulers sought to establish Islam as the religion of India. This process, though never completed, occasioned much strife and tension among the native population.

"There is but one God whose name is true, the Creator, devoid of fear and enmity, immortal, unborn, self-existent; by the favor of the Guru."

—*The Adi Granth*

Guru Nanak

It was into these circumstances that in the year 1469 an Indian named Nanak was born. A member of one of the lower castes, Nanak was the son of a shepherd. From his youth, Nanak was a dreamer, who frequently was the object of his father's anger as the result of his losing a goat or two. Nanak would get caught up in his thoughts, as he watched the fleecy clouds drift along, unaware that some of the herd was wandering off. His head was full of ideas, many of them concerning religious concepts. Nanak's best friend, despite the disapproval of his parents, was a young Moslem named Kabir. He and Kabir would while away their free time together discussing the differences between their two religions.

Because these two young men respected and loved one another, they wondered why religion should come between them. They were all too familiar with the strife which religious differences caused among their people. They reasoned that ultimately Allah and Brahma were one and the same and the two distinct religions were merely two different approaches to the same God, different only because they originated among different peoples. Nanak admired many of the teachings of Islam and Kabir, too, found much to admire in his friend's religion. They dreamed together of a kind of religious compromise which would end the tension and division in their country.

The Compromise

As their religious ideas began to jell, some ideas from Hinduism, some from Islam were retained, while others were rejected. To this combination were added some of their own, original ideas. The product of this compromise became the basis for the new religion which Nanak founded. From Hinduism was drawn the concept of karma, the belief in a moral imperative given each person, together with the obligation to fulfill that duty. The idea of reincarnation, tied so closely to karma was also retained: a person's next life would be his reward or his punishment for actions in his present life. The caste system was rejected: all men and women are equal in God's eyes. A respect for all forms of life expressed in vegetarianism was also preserved. From Islam came the belief in one God, a strict monotheism devoid of even the slightest suggestion of other gods or manifestations of the godhead. Even the idea of angels, very much a part of Islam, was eliminated for fear that some would misinterpret them as minor deities. The idea of equality which supplanted the caste came from Islam as well. The compromise did away with the concept of priesthood, an essential element in Hindu worship, but absent in Islam. Another Islamic idea, that of militarism, the willingness to fight for one's religious freedom, was also adopted. The prohibition against the use of intoxicating beverages is likewise derived from Moslem practice. The original ideas of Nanak and Kabir will become apparent as the distinctive features of Sikhism are discussed.

These are the religious ideas that Nanak began to preach to his friends and neighbors. The style of his proselytizing efforts, reminiscent of the Old West's "medicine shows" is worth noting. He and Kabir had a young friend, a Hindu boy named Mordana, who had a gift for singing. They would have Mordana begin to sing on a street corner of a village or city, and when a crowd had been attracted by the free concert, Nanak would then step forward and begin to preach his new religion. One must assume that part of the appeal had to be Nanak's call for universal brotherhood and an end to religious strife. And yet, undeniably, some of its appeal may well have been the new faith's rejection of the burden of the caste. This appeal was evident in the popularity of Buddhism as well.

The Sikh Religion Draws Ideas From:		
Hinduism	**and**	**Islam**
Deism		Monotheism
Karma		Equality
Rebirth		No Priests
Non-Violence		Militarism
Vegetarianism		No Alchohol

The Ten Gurus

As the movement gained converts, Nanak began to be called "Guru," a term that simply means "religous teacher." It is not certain just how many followers he had by the time of his death, but it is known that when he died, his followers, known as "Nanakpanthis," literally followers of Nanak, decided to elect in his place another guru. Apparently the mogul rulers did not feel threatened by this as yet small and harmless group of religious innovators, and so down through the years until the Fifth Guru, Arjun Dev, the Nanakpanthis continued to grow in numbers, preserving their unique identity as a new religion, in relative peace.

Guru Arjun is remembered by Sikhs for several reasons. Being a gifted writer himself, he decided to gather together the fragments of writings attributed to Nanak and his other three predecessors. He edited them, adding a significant portion of his own words, into a book that was simply titled "The Book" or *Granth*. This work, which is sometimes referred to as the *Adi Granth* or the *Granth Sahib,* became the sacred book of the Sikh religion. It has assumed a crucial role in the religion, as will be seen shortly. Arjun is also remembered for establishing the city of Amritsar in the Punjab as the center of the new religion, building there a beautiful temple called the Golden Temple because of its gilt dome. This display of strength and independence may have alarmed the moguls. The climate of religious tolerance which had prevailed in the early years of the new religion's existence now changed to one of persecution. Perhaps for this reason, Guru Arjun built his temple on a tank of water 500 feet square, designing access to the temple only by drawbridge. The Golden Temple became therefore not only a place of worship and center of pilgrimage but also a fortification in which Sikhs could find safety. Arjun counseled his people to resist persecution and not to hesitate to arm themselves to defend their religious freedom.

Between the death of Guru Arjun and that of the tenth Guru, Gobind Singh, the Sikhs came under repeated attack for their religious beliefs. This tenth Guru became disgusted with those of his people who in the face of violence denied their fatih, committing the shameful sin of apostasy. He ordered that henceforth all adult male Sikhs would be required to observe strict rules of dress and grooming, and in this way demonstrate their willingness to profess their faith publicly.

The Five Kukkas

There rules are known as the Laws of *Khalsa* and include the Five Kukkas. The word kukka stands for the letter "k" and is used because each of the Laws of Khalsa begin with that letter. The first of these is *kes,* by which all male members are forbidden to ever cut their hair, whether facial, head, or body hair. This necessitates the wearing of a head covering at all times. Most Sikhs wear turbans on their heads. All Sikh men must wear a *kunga* or wooden comb to keep their hair neatly in place under their head-covering. Each Sikh likewise must wear a pair of *kachas* or white drawers in place of the traditional dhoti or toga-like robe most Indians of the time wore. Next, each Sikh was to wear on his right arm a wide bracelet made of steel called a *kara.* Lastly, each was to carry at all times a double-edged dagger called a *khanda* or *khirpan,* depending on its length. One can see that each of these prescriptions for dress are intended to keep every adult male prepared to fight. Even to this day Sikhs, wherever they are living, observe the Laws of Khalsa very strictly. If a Sikh should so much as cut his hair or shave in order to accommodate himself to a different culture, he is considered to have committed the grave sin of apostasy, and he is shunned by other Sikhs.

By the time of Guru Gobind Singh, the guruship had become a hereditary institution with each guru passing on the position to his eldest son. Gobind Singh had lost each of his three sons in battles fought against the moguls. When his own death approached, he directed that there be no guru after him. "Let the Granth be your Guru," he commanded. And so it has been ever since. Gobind Singh was the last of the ten gurus to lead the Sikhs. He is remembered for more than the Five Kukkas or for being the last guru, however. So beloved was he by his people that in his memory every male Sikh is named Singh, at least as a middle name. In addition, after the death of Guru Gobind Singh, the followers of this new faith were no longer called Nanakpanthis, or followers of Nanak, but became Sikhs, meaning "disciples." In all probability he was the greatest of all the gurus.

Sikh Worship

Among all the religions of the East, Sikh worship is probably the most unique. Not only is it a monotheistic worship, honoring the one true God, known as *Ek Unkar* or "The Name," but it is also a worship which is focused on a Holy Book, The Granth. In each Sikh temple an ornate copy of the Granth is kept in a secure place and then brought out for the service and placed upon an elaborate pedestal or throne covered always by a canopy. No other part of the temple is decorated. Liturgical music is always monophonic so as not to distract from the sacred presence. The Granth is the center of worship. Following the Islamic custom, shoes are always removed before entering the temple. Worshippers approach the Granth and reverence it before taking their places. At marriages the bride and groom circle the Granth three times, signifying their acknowledgment of this divine presence which sanctifies their union. Readings are done in a sequential cycle so that the entire book is proclaimed several times during each year. Children are brought to the service for a naming ceremony, and they always receive a name which begins with the same letter of the first word of that day's reading from the Granth, signifying that their name is given by God. At the conclusion of the service, the Holy Book is ceremoniously returned to its place of safe-keeping. For Sikhs today the Granth is truly their Guru.

The Sikhs And British Colonialism

The British presence in India had begun in the Sixteenth Century, during the reign of Queen Elizabeth I, with the mercantile inroads of the East India Company, a private corporation chartered and supported by the Crown. To consolidate its foothold in India and to guarantee the safety and success of its trade, the Company employed its own army. It was strong enough to take possession of some important coastal cities like Calcutta. Shortly after the Napoleonic Wars at the beginning of the Nineteenth Century, Britain had placed more than half of the sub- continent under its direct rule, and ruled the rest indirectly through puppet local maharajahs who were allowed to exercise limited autonomy.

Musicians called ragis perform during a Sikh service. Women take an active part in religious services whether at home or in the temple.

The Sikhs in the Punjab had provided the strongest opposition to the British conquest, but in the year 1849 they too were defeated. The British were so impressed with the valor and fighting skills of this separatist minority in northwest India, they signed a treaty with its leader, one Dalip Singh, which arranged a mercenary relationship between the conquerors and the conquered. The Sikhs were paid to fight along side the British against their fellow countrymen, the Hindus and the Moslems. Needless to say, they had no qualms about fighting the moguls who had persecuted them off and on for three hundred years. This arrangement lasted into the Twentieth Century when in 1947 Britain granted independence to India, seeking to prevent religious wars between Hindus and Moslems by partitioning the country into Hindu India and Moslem Pakistan. Unfortunately this arrangement did nothing to secure the religious and political rights of the Sikhs. This background explains much of the tension between Sikhs in the Punjab and the Hindu majority government in New Delhi.

Sikh Violence Today

In recent years there has been a great deal of tension in India between the Hindu majority and the Sikhs. The roots of this problem go all the way back to the Sikh religious community's alliance with the British Raj. In more recent times, however, they may be traced to the partition of India when independence was granted. The intention was to avoid a religious blood-bath between the Hindu and Moslem populations. The Punjab, home to the vast majority of the world's Sikhs, was left as one of the many states of the new India. This state included a Sikh majority in the central and northern parts, and a Hindu minority in the south. Ironically, Nanak's birthplace is located in the south, and so there is a constant movement of Sikhs making pilgrimages into that part of the state, making it a hotspot for friction and potential conflict.

A second cause of this ongoing tension is the Sikh's dream for independence, or at least autonomy within the Punjab. Like any other large group of individuals, Sikhs include conservatives, moderates, and extremists. Sikh extremists are inclined to believe that there is no way they will ever realize their dream of independence without resorting to violence. The union of both religious and patriotic feelings, as has been demonstrated in other parts of the world, makes for an extremely volatile faction. On several occasions in recent years there have been outbreaks of violence in which the Prime Minister in New Delhi was forced to send in the army to restore law and order. In June of 1984, extremists, who had committed acts of terrorism against the Hindu population of the Punjab, sought sanctuary in the Golden Temple. The army was ordered to assault the Temple and in the process killed a large number of these terrorists. This violation of their holy place angered even moderate Sikhs.

The tension continues to grow between these two religions. Because of their long tradition of military prowess, Sikhs have always occupied positions of trust and authority in the army. Though comprising only two percent of the total population of India, Sikhs make up twenty percent of the army. Two of them were acting as guards at the residence of Indira Gandhi, the Prime Minister, in November of 1984. One morning, as she made her way from the residence to her office in another part of the compound, probably in retaliation for the June attack on the Golden Temple, these Sikh guards assassinated her.

Though there may be no easy solution to this conflict in the near future, reaching a state of peaceful coexistence remains a high priority for the Indian government.

Questions For Review

1. How is the origin of the Sikh religion different from any of the other religions studied so far?

2. Describe both the political and religious situation in India at the time Guru Nanak lived.

3. Summarize the basic ideas in Sikhism, indicating those ideas derived from Hinduism, those from Islam, and those that might be considered original.

4. Describe the changes in Sikh beliefs and traditions as the religion evolved over its first hundred years, under the leadership of the Ten Gurus.

5. Make a list of all those features of Sikhism which you consider unique among the Indian religions studied thus far.

6. Identify: guru, mogul, Punjab, Amritsar, the Golden Temple, Guru Arjun Dev, the Granth, Guru Gobind Singh, the kukkas, Nanakpanthis, syncretism.

3

Religions Of The Orient

"At fifteen my mind was fixed on learning. By thirty my character had been formed. At forty I had no more confusions. At fifty I understood the mandate of Heaven. At sixty it was easy for me to hear the truth. At seventy I could follow my desire without transgressing what was right."

—*The Analects*

Confucianism

At first glance, Confucianism does not appear to be a religion at all. There are no gods, no creeds, no sacraments, no holy books as such. It may even be argued that Confucius, its founder, never intended to establish a religion. One might wonder, therefore, how it can be considered a religion. To answer this objection, it is helpful to remember that there are two dimensions of religion, the vertical and the horizontal. By the vertical dimension of religion is meant one's individual relationship to God or the gods. By the horizontal is meant one's relationships to one's neighbors, the social dimension of religion. Both are important. Confucianism does not deny the vertical; it merely emphasizes the horizontal. And it does so by perpetuating a solemn code of ethics which, if observed, will bring about peace and harmony on earth.

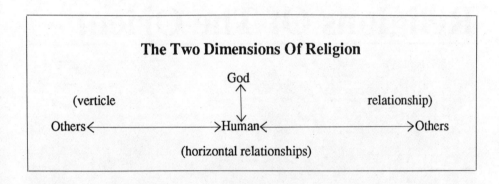

The Two Dimensions Of Religion

God

(verticle   relationship)

Others ←—————————→ Human ←—————————→ Others

(horizontal relationships)

Primitive Chinese Religions

China is probably the oldest continuous civilization on earth. According to the theory of the evolution of religion mentioned in Chapter One, the first expression of religious consciousness was probably pantheism, the belief that the sacred is to be found everywhere, in all of creation, and all creation is sacred. One of the manifestations of pantheistic belief is animism, the idea that all living beings possess a spirit, and this spirit being immaterial is not bound by earthly, physical limitations; it is therefore sacred. If Confucianism has any claim to being a real religion, it is probably best interpreted as an animistic religion. Indeed one of the earliest forms of Chinese religion was ancestor-worship, the practice of honoring the members of one's family who live on after death in the spirit-world. Confucius not only venerated his own ancestors, but he glorified the past in which they lived, teaching that in the past everything was peaceful and harmonious because the ancients knew how to live right. If humanity experiences any suffering or failure, it is because it has ceased to observe the ways of the past.

The Life And Times Of K'ung Fu-Tse

The name Confucius is not Chinese. It is a Latinization of the Chinese *K'ung Fu-Tse,* which means K'ung the learned master. His name may have been first Latinized by the famous Jesuit missionary, Father Mateo Ricci. Ricci was sent to China by Ignatius Loyola himself. When he arrived there, he was very impressed with the Chinese people and their ancient culture. It did not take Ricci long to develop an appreciation for Confucius and his place in the hearts of the Chinese. They venerated him in the same way that Christians venerated the saints. And so Father Ricci used Confucius as an example of the kind of righteous living called for by the Gospel he was preaching. It is said that Ricci even included Confucius' name at the commemoration of the saints in the Mass.

K'ung was born in the Sixth Century, B.C. in northeast China in the Province of Lu, located at the base of the Shantung Peninsula, just south of the present capitol, Beijing. As with so many other religious figures of the past, historians are not sure of very many details of his life. The story of Confucius is a mixture of fact and fiction. Some of the details seem indisputable; others are at best questionable. Here is one of the versions of his life.

Ch'iu K'ung was an only child, son of a military man named Heigh, who was the highest ranking officer in the provincial army. His father died when he was only a small boy, but because of his father's position, the provincial govenor guaranteed the welfare of Confucius and his widowed mother, even to the point of underwriting his education. When Confucius had completed his schooling, the governor found him a job in the civil service of the province. He soon rose in the ranks and was appointed director of granaries, a position of considerable importance in a country dependent on rice as its staple crop. Even to this day China's fickle climate plays havoc with its food supply. In years of average rainfall, there is plenty to eat for everyone, but in years of drought, famine is common. One of Confucius' first acts as director was to raise the province tax on farmers, a very unpopular move. He doubled the number of bushels of rice per acre required as tax, and he stored this surplus in the government's granaries. A few years later famine struck China, but the Province of Lu had enough rice to feed all of its citizens. Confucius was praised for his wisdom and foresight, and he became an instant hero.

Around this time Confucius' mother died. In keeping with the Chinese custom of extended mourning for the death of one's parents, he requested the govenor's permission to resign his position and retire from public life. By this time he had married and was the father of a young son named Leigh. Together with his family, Confucius began a three year period of mourning, neither socializing with his friends, nor even going out of the house. He used this quiet time of his life to return to the life of a student which he loved so well. He began to collect ancient works of Chinese literature, sifting through them for the wisdom of the past. By the end of his official mourning period he had collected quite a library of classics, and he had become something of a scholar. As the mourning drew to a close, he often invited guests into his home for long dinner parties, featuring philosophical dialogues that were sometimes more like monologues. His friends were impressed with his wisdom and knowledge and urged him to teach. They promised to send Confucius their sons as soon as he opened an academy. This he did, glad to have the opportunity to continue his scholarly pursuits. Soon his home was filled with young men seeking an education. Confucius used his library of classic Chinese literature as his basic curriculum.

Confucius probably would have been quite happy to spend the rest of his life as a teacher: he had found his niche in life. But this was not to be. Duty called, when the governor decided he needed Confucius' management skills to deal with a grave problem facing the province: a crime wave. Confucius was asked to accept the position of director of prisons. When one recalls that it was this same governor who had provided so generously for both him and his mother following his father's death, it is not so surprising that Confucius would give up what had become so important to him to respond to the call to service. On assuming his new position and first studying the problem of crime in Lu, he concluded that the reason why men became criminals was their inability to do anything else. They were uneducated and knew no trade, so they stole what they needed. Confucius directed that every inmate in prison be required to attend classes, learning a trade in prison workshops. This not only reduced the cost to the province of supporting the prisons, since the items produced in the workshops could be sold to the public, but it also assured the convicts of the ability to support themselves when released. In a few short years the crime wave in Lu was eliminated and the prison population reduced to a handful of hardened criminals. Once again Confucius had solved a serious problem using practical wisdom, a wisdom he humbly attributed to the golden age of the past.

This most recent triumph drew the admiration of the Emperor himself in Beijing, who decided that Confucius, this practical genius from Lu, would make the ideal tutor for his eldest son, the crown prince. And so, once again Confucius answered the call to service. He moved his family to the Capitol and into the heavenly palace. His lone student was so captivated by his new tutor that he begged his father to invite him to dinner. The Emperor knew at once that he had made the right choice for his son who would one day succeed him as emperor. Soon he was consulting his son's tutor about his own problems. This must have gratified Confucius greatly, and made his sacrificing the academy seem somehow worthwhile, if he could have some influence at this highest level of government. Soon Confucius was the principal advisor to the Emperor, thereby earning the envy and hatred of other members of the imperial council. These disgruntled councilors decided to try to disgrace this newcomer, but they soon learned that Confucius' conduct was above reproach. They then turned to distracting the Emperor from his new advisor, an attempt that proved to be more realistic. These jealous men purchased for the Emperor gifts of race horses and dancing girls in the hope that he would be so occupied with these frivolous diversions that he would have no time for affairs of state. Their plan worked, and soon Confucius became so disgusted with the ruler's inattention to duty that he resigned his position and returned to Lu. Back home, somewhat disenchanted with government service, he reopened his beloved academy. Soon he was educating the sons of the wealthy and powerful from all over northeast China. He may have hoped he could affect the nation's destiny through its future leaders. At any rate, it was in this role that he spent the remaining years of his life.

The Classics

The legacy which Confucius bequeathed to China was not so much in the form of a religion as much as it was a system of educating the young to the ways of the ancients. All his life Confucius had attempted to share his love for the wisdom of past ages, which he had discovered for himself in the classics. The writings which he selected as the basic curriculum for the students at his academy were the means he chose to communicate the values he held sacred. It must be understood that Confucius was largely responsible for preserving these writings, many of which he must have found only in fragments. By editing them into a standard collection, deleting here, adding on there, Confucius was able to weave together the fabric of his moral philosophy for living.

The collection is usually divided into two categories. The first is known as the *Wu Ching* or the Five Classics. It is not important to know each of these works by name. They contain history, chronicles of warriors and kings, poetry, court ritual and

China: 1027-300 B.C.E.

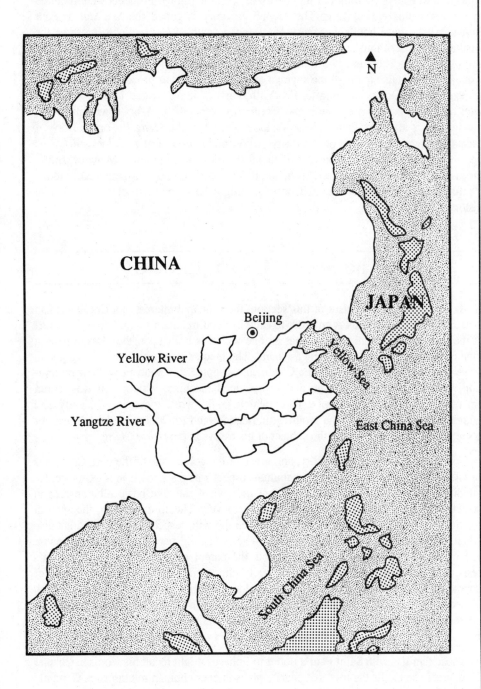

ceremony, even augury. By far the most important of these is the *Hsiao Ching* or the Book of Filial Piety. Some scholars believe Confucius himself was its author. It is a collection of essays spelling out the theory of social harmony. Students were required to memorize this entire work. The second category is called the *Ssu Shu* or Four Books. All of these books were written after the death of Confucius to preserve the wisdom of his teaching at the academy. They deal with law, political theory, ethics, and philosophy. There are two that bear special mention. The first is the Analects, a work which contains many of the sayings of the Master. It was probably written by the students of Confucius shortly after his death. Parts of it are written in dialogue form, with a student posing a question and Confucius responding. A book written over a hundred years after Confucius is also included here. It is the *Meng Tze* or the Book of Mencius. Mencius was one of the many philosophers who idealized Confucius. This book represents an elaboration on the social theories of Confucius. Mencius, sometimes called "the Second Master," is generally credited with popularizing what is today Confucianism. Without Mencius, Confucius might be merely a footnote in Chinese history.

The Secret Of Happiness

As mentioned at the outset of this section, the principal interest that Confucius had was the reordering of society in order to establish and maintain social harmony. China at the time was a feudal society, that is, one which is built upon the class system, a kind of a caste, as much economic as social. The inequality of its citizens was a given: some men were superior to others. Confucius accepted this concept without reservation, viewing society as a large and complicated machine, which, if it was to run smoothly, required finely tuned parts which could work together efficiently and without friction. Any machine requires lubrication, and to Confucius the lubricant of society was "mutual respect," the subject of his essays in the *Hsiao Ching*.

To recapture the peace, gentility, and grace of the golden age of the past, Confucius insisted that the virtue of "hsiao" or mutual respect was paramount in importance. He taught that this is the essential ingredient in each of the five basic relationships in society, the Five *Lun,* if harmony is to be achieved. The first of these, the spousal relationship, will be harmonious not only when the wife respects her husband but also when the husband respects and honors his wife. The child-parent relationship likewise requires mutual respect: the child respects the parent as a response to the parent's respecting the child. Beyond the family unity, the young must respect their elders, of course, but this must come as a result of older citizens treating those younger with respect. The employee and his employer must also render mutual respect to one another, if their relationship is to be harmonious. Finally, each citizen must respect his ruler, but this respect must be reciprocated by rulers who treat their subjects kindly.

Those familiar with Saint Paul's Letter to Ephesus might recall his words in Chapter Five, where he exalts the role that charity plays in every human relationship. Certainly the sentiments are the same, though for Saint Paul the motivation is quite different: Christians love and respect one another not simply to create harmonious relationships, but "for the sake of the Lord."

For over twenty-five hundred years this principle of mutual respect guaranteed a remarkable stability in Chinese society. Friction between the classes was practically unknown. Corruption in the bureaucracy was at a minimum, and members of the vast civil service were both capable and efficient. Since eligibility for government employment was based on public examination in the classics, one might conclude that the political theories of Confucius were largely responsible.

Confucius had quite a bit to say about good government in his writings. He felt very strongly that rulers should, perhaps more than any others, develop and nurture the classic virtues of benevolence, righteousness, propriety, wisdom, and sincerity. His own experience with rulers had been somewhat disappointing. In his own version of a caste system he placed the scholar at the head of society. Next came the farmer, for, as the scholar feeds the intellectual life of a person, the farmer feeds his body. Then comes the artisan who creates both beautiful and useful things out of the raw materials of the earth. And lastly, he places the merchant who acts as a middleman in the exchange of goods. Curiously, he makes no place for soldiers or politicians.

Confucius And Religion

One might ask if Confucius had anything at all to say about religion in his writings. He certainly was no atheist, but, in accord with the tenor of his times, he might be considered something of an agnostic. He does not deny the existence of the supernatural order. He merely suggests that he is so taken up with dealing with the things of this world that he has little time to consider the things of heaven. This concept of "Heaven" is one which was commonly used in his time to refer to the supernatural, a kind of limitless, impersonal "ultimate cause" of the philosophers. Heaven was to be worshipped, but primarily by the head of state, as he alone was in a position to relate to this august reality. Perhaps the term "deist" best decribes Confucius' thoughts on religion. The deist believes that there is a God who creates, but that this God thereafter has little to do with creatures as individual persons. They are on their own, as it were.

Confucius And The New China

It should be evident by now that Confucius was a conservative in the strictest sense of that word: he wished above all to conserve all the values he perceived in the golden age of humanity. In his mind this was the only way to achieve harmony among men. For this reason it should come as no surprise that the leaders of the revolution in twentieth century China had no use for him or his traditional thinking. Mao Tse-Tung, the father of communist China, once said:

> "I hated Confucius from the age of eight...Emphasis on honoring
> Confucius and the reading of the classics, along with advocacy of the
> old rules of propriety and education and philosophy, are part of that
> semi-feudal culture..." (which must be overthrown).

China, under Mao's leadership, underwent a host of drastic changes which came to be called "the cultural revolution." The old values canonized by Confucius were totally rejected. In Mao's eyes the ways of the past had led only to injustice and class distinctions. They had only served to maintain China as "the sleeping giant" among the world's great nations. He felt the time had come for the giant to awaken and take its rightful place in the rapidly changing times of the Twentieth Century.

And so, the Learned Master has not fared well in modern China. The communist government there has attempted to eliminate his influence from society, an influence that lasted for over twenty-five hundred years. This effort was symbolized with one of the first acts of this new government in the public burning of Confucianist literature. Today the memory and the heritage of Confucius is kept alive and well in Taiwan, formerly the island of Formosa, where hundreds of thousands of nationalists, who had fought against the communists and lost, fled in 1949.

Questions For Review

1. Separate the facts from the fiction in the story of Confucius. How much is really known about him?

2. How would you answer the often heard objection that Confucianism is not really a religion at all?

3. According to Confucius, what is the key to social harmony? How does it work?

4. Describe the impact which Confucius had on Chinese society down through history.

5. After the victory of the communist forces in 1949, Confucianism ceased to be a part of Chinese life. Why was that?

6. Identify: K'ung Fu-Tse, Lu, Wu Ching, Ssu Shu, hsiao, Analects, Mencius.

Taoism

One of the things that is difficult for westerners to understand about eastern religions is that in general they are very tolerant of divergent views. The name Catholic came to Christianity early on in its history as the result of the development of heresies or divergent views. Actually it was the Emperor Constantine who insisted on uniformity in the Church's teachings, calling the Council of Nicea to set forth "catholic" doctrine, that is, an interpretation that would be upheld universally throughout the Church. Eastern religions rarely insist on such a normative interpretation, and in some cases allow their members to embrace more than one faith. To these religions, if one belief is good, two is even better.

The place of Taoism among Chinese religions is a further indication of this eclectic approach. In China one does not find some dedicated to Confucianism and others to Taoism, so much as one sees each person making use of several religions, usually for different purposes or on different occasions. In China there are actually three religions common among its people. The two native religions of Confucianism and Taoism are practiced, as well as Buddhism, brought from India by Bodhidharma and other missionary- monks. There religions do not seem to compete; rather they complement one another. In the days prior to the communist revolution, it was common that the young would be educated in the principles of Confucianism, married in a Taoist ceremony, and buried at a service led by a Buddhist monk.

If Confucianism reflects the primitive pantheistic belief in animism, then it might be said that Taoism reflects the equally primitive pantheistic belief in naturism. From the very origins of their civilization, the Chinese have always reverenced nature, and seen in its dynamic forces something sacred. This very early consciousness of the sacred power of nature endures in Taoism even today.

The Legend Of Lao-Tse

The story of Lao-Tse is somewhat reminiscent of that of Mahavira, the founder of Jainism, inasmuch as very little is known about him. So little, in fact, that many comparative religion scholars agree that he may never have lived. He too may be the work of myth-makers who wanted to create a personality who would rival the immortal Confucius. All that is known about him is an episode which is supposed to have occurred toward the end of his life.

"There was something containing all, before heaven and earth it exists...Alone it stands and does not change. It goes everywhere and is not hindered. It can thereby become the universe's mother. I know not its name; I characterize it by calling it the Way."

—*Tao Tei Ching*

A Taoist monk meets visitors at a mountain retreat near Hua Qing, China.

We meet Lao-Tse, whose name means "the venerable old philosopher," at the age of seventy-two. He is the archivist in a province of northeast China some time in the Sixth Century, B.C. Apparently he has worked in the civil service all his life. Over the years he has read all of the classics of Chinese literature and in the process has become a great scholar. For some reason he becomes disgusted with the local ruler, and he decides to resign his position and leave the province. As he is leaving, he is stopped by a guard at the gate who recognizes him. Upon questioning him, the guard refuses to allow him to leave the province. He tells Lao-Tse that the only way he could allow the wisest citizen of the province to leave would be if he could write down everything he knows in a book. This Lao-Tse agrees to do, and three days later hands over to the guard a book he has entitled the *Tao Tei Ching* or the Book of the Way of Virtue. The guard accepts the book and allows him to leave. Lao-Tse is never heard of again.

Historians wonder which came first, the book or the author. Many suggest that the *Tao Tei Ching* is a timeless classic of Chinese literature, which is more likely the work of several anonymous authors rather than one. This work, they conjecture, became so influential among certain later scholars and philosophers that an attempt was made to attribute it to one single scholar of the same rank as Confucius. Thus began the legend of the scholar and the gatekeeper. It is the essence of this book which became the foundation for "philosophical Taoism."

More Syncretism

Taoism itself is actually the result of a fusion of two systems of thought, one philosophical and one religious. The philosophical ideas found in *Tao Tei Ching*, dating from the Sixth Century, B.C. were later combined with some purely religious concepts arising from primitive Chinese naturism around the Sixth Century of the Christian Era to produce what is called "religious Taoism." If in fact Lao-Tse really did exist, it is highly doubtful that he would recognize or, for that matter, approve of the religion which names him as its founder. The process whereby this fusion of traditions took place may be described as an example of syncretism, but not so much of the conscious or deliberate variety. The transition was too gradual to be calculated.

The Tao

Despite the academic background attributed to Lao-Tse, the *Tao Tei Ching* is quite anti-intellectual. It is as if he were saying that, after all he had learned from the classics, he had concluded that all this knowledge was superfluous. True wisdom is found not in the accumulation of knowledge but in discovering the *Tao*. By Tao he means "the way things are and ought to be." It is the Law of Nature, the ultimate principle which governs life. To know this reality and to accomodate oneself to its ways is the key to happiness. Irrational creatures do this through a sense of instinct: and they are unquestionably happy and at peace. Humanity fails to find lasting happiness because they attempt to master nature, to circumvent its laws. Humans fight nature, thinking their rationality will give them the edge. To be happy, all humanity must do is find their place in nature and follow the Tao.

The *Tao Tei Ching* teaches that life is really very simple if one observes the Tao. No special effort is required. People need only arrange their lives in harmony with the Way, only being careful not to act against the Tao. This notion of non-interference is called *wu-wei,* literally "not-doing." It does not suggest non-action, but rather the

Yin-Yang

avoidance of trying too hard, attempting to rise above nature. Know your place, and keep it. This classic also recommends that humanity live simply. Civilization is the ruination of mankind. The less complicated one's life remains, the happier one will be. Moreover, the accumulation of wealth and material possessions will only cause envy among others, and thus disrupt social harmony. Christians may be reminded of these words of Jesus in his Sermon on the Mount:

> "Look at the birds in the sky. They do not sow or reap or gather into barns; yet your heavenly Father feeds them... Think of the flowers growing in the fields; they never have to work or spin; yet not even Solomon in all his regalia was ever robed like one of these..." (Mt 6:26,28).

Yin-Yang

The symbol chosen by philosophical Taoism to represent one's adherence to the Law of Tao is that of *Yin-Yang*, a closed circle evenly divided by a gradual s-shaped line into two equal parts, one dark, the other light. This symbol is used to connote the "give-and-take" aspect of life. Life is neither all black nor all white, but a smooth ebb and flow between the two. *Yin-Yang* symbolizes the fact that life itself is a union of opposites. Yin is cold, but Yang is warm; Yin is dark, Yang light; Yin is passive, Yang active; Yin is negative, Yang positive; Yin is female, Yang male; Yin is evil, Yang good. It must be noted here that the reference to evil refers only to what might be called "physical evil," and certainly not moral evil. Examples of physical evil include things like disease, natural calamity, even death from natural causes. Both Yin and Yang are good, morally speaking. For Lao-Tse the only moral evil is to resist the Tao, to fight against it. Harmony in music is sometimes the result of the blending of discordant sounds; harmony in life is likewise found in the balance between opposites. True happiness may be found only in one's complete resignation to this fact of life. While Confucianism teaches that one must create harmony through his own efforts, Taoism teaches that one need only discover harmony through finding one's balance in a world of opposites.

The Dualism Of Yin-Yang

Yin	Yang
Dark ⟵——————————⟶	Light
Cold ⟵——————————⟶	Warm
Negative ⟵——————————⟶	Positive
Passive ⟵——————————⟶	Active
Female ⟵——————————⟶	Male
Evil ⟵——————————⟶	Good

Taoism And Confucianism

There is obviously a high degree of contrast between these two Chinese philosophies. While Confucianism appears to be very much man-centered, Taoism seems to be centered in nature. Confucius sees man as the master of the earth, at the pinnacle of the created world. Taoism sees man as just one more part of creation. Instead of the pyramid with man at the top, it has man as part of the circle of life-forms, each dependent on one another, and none of them superior. So marked is this contrast that some scholars suggest that Taoism may even have arisen as a reaction to Confucianism's activist approach to life.

Whereas Confucianism is concerned with the public good, Taoism concentrates on the individual. Confucianism teaches gentility and etiquette; Taoism encourages spontaneity and freedom. While Confucianism is interested in preserving the status quo, Taoism is comfortable with the state of flux. And finally, though Confucianism strives for a final triumph, Taoism is prepared to accept defeat along with victory.

Consider the metaphor of a man crossing a raging river. Confucianist tactics might call for him to dive in and fight the current, struggling to reach the opposite bank. Taoism, on the other hand might have him walk upstream a short way, then swim diagonally with the current until he reaches the other side. By using the force of nature, and not fighting against it, man achieves his goal without a struggle, and without the danger of not surviving the task. This is what is meant by the doctrine of *wu-wei:* it is not passivity, but rather activity which does not violate the way things ought to be— the *Tao*.

Still another way of appreciating the differences between the two philosophies may be the opposition between the industrialist and the environmentalist. If the Confucianist is building a road and comes up to a mountain, he might tunnel through the mountain, since a straight line is the shortest distance between two points. The Taoist, however, respecting the integrity of the mountain, will simply lay out his road the long way, going around the mountain.

Confucius and Lao Tse: A Contrast In Approaches	
Confucius	**Lao Tse**
Concerned with the Community	Concerned with the Individual
Taught Gentility & Respect for tradition	Taught Freedom & Spontaneity
Emphasized Citizenship and Good Government	Emphasized Independence and Relating to Nature
Considered Human Beings to be the Master of Nature	Considered Human Beings to be merely a Part of Nature
More or less ignored the gods	Saw the gods as expressions of the Forces of Nature

The Evolution Of Taoism

As mentioned earlier, philosophical Taoism was fused with naturistic religious elements native to China some time around the Sixth Century, A.D. The way this came about is not known for certain, but many scholars suggest this development had something to do with the advent of Buddhist monasticism. It was about this time that monasteries of Chinese monks who were not Buddhists, but who were apparently influenced by Buddhism, began to appear. These monks adopted the common lifestyle and the habit of common prayer and meditation which they witnessed in Buddhist monasteries, but with a uniquely Chinese religion, one based on the commentaries on philosophical Taoism. The monks were obsessed with the mystical power of the *Tao*, and they sought to discover ways to make use of that power. They firmly believed that, if one could only discover the way, one might possess great powers, even obtain immortality. Many of the more primitive concepts of naturism, such as the divination of spirits, exorcism, alchemy, and magic, found their way into this brotherhood. There is some evidence to suggest that due to the secrecy of their practices and the ever increasing influence which these monks exerted, they suffered persecution from the government and in response originated certain forms of the martial arts which are still practiced today.

Dualism Or Polytheism?

There are in Taoism the twin principles of Yin and Yang. Does this mean that it is a dualistic religion? There is also in Taoism the cult of various gods and goddesses. Is this proof that Taoism is instead polytheistic? Though the dualistic nature of the Yin-Yang concept is undeniable, it must be remembered that this notion originated more as a philosophical interpretation of reality than a theological one. In addition, the impersonal nature of these principles might be more indicative of pantheism than dualism. With regard to the deity-worship found in Taoism, once again it may be, like the many gods of Hinduism, which seem to fill the need for personal gods, more suggestive of pantheism than polytheism. Perhaps the best response to the question raised is neither. Despite the fact that sometimes religions mean different things to different people, Taoism, like Confucianism, probably has much more to do with man and his relationship to the world around him than with God.

The Taoist Influence On Zen Buddhism

It is interesting to note the influence that Taoism exercised on the Chinese phase of the evolution of Zen Buddhism. Several key ideas found in Zen today may be attibuted to Taoism. For example, the use of paradox as the subject of meditation is inherent in the Taoist concept of Yin-Yang as the union of opposites and apparent contradictions. The idea of gentle and yielding firmness in the swordsmanship and archery techniques of the samurai warriors who practiced Zen may be traced to the doctrine of *wu-wei*. The aesthetic sense of simplicity and uncomplicated beauty as seen in the Zen styling of gardens and floral arrangements may also have been influenced by the Taoist reverence for nature. Most important of all, the Zen notion of *satori* seems to reflect the anti-intellectualism of Taoism.

Once again, one is reminded of the amazing complementarity of these oriental religions. They do not always exclude ideas other religions project, but in fact frequently find great compatibility in the very multiplicity of religious expressions.

Questions For Review

1. How much is actually known about the founder of Taoism, Lao- Tse?

2. Is Taoism the same today that it was when it was founded?

3. What is meant by the Taoist symbol of the Yin-Yang?

4. According to the *Tao Tei Ching*, what is man's principal duty in life?

5. Sum up the ways that Taoism differs from Confucianism.

6. Which religion, Confucianism or Taoism, posed a greater threat to the communist philosophy espoused by Mao Tse-Tung? Why?

7. Identify: Yin-Yang, Tao Tei Ching, Tao, wu-wei.

Father and daughter are praying to influence the "way of the spirits."

Shinto

The religion most closely associated with Japan is Shinto. The name itself says something about its origins, for it is a combination of two Chinese words, *shen*, meaning "spirits," and *tao*, meaning "the way." The Japanese version is *kami no richi*. The word *kami* means spirit and more will be said about that concept in what follows. Since the name of the most typical Japanese religion is itself Chinese, one can assume that Chinese religions had at least something to do with the development of the religion called "the way of the spirits."

The fact that its own religious expressions were significantly influenced by Chinese religion is in no way surprising, considering the fact that practically every other aspect of Japanese culture came under that same influence. Japan was regarded by the Chinese in the same way that Sixteenth Century Europeans regarded the Americas. It was a land of new frontiers and strange inhabitants who were considered inferior to the Chinese. The first excursions made from mainland China to the islands of Japan probably began around the year 500 with explorers most likely looking for trade opportunities. Soon, more than goods were being exported: the thrust of Chinese language, alphabet, art, architecture, philosophy, and religion impacted on the comparatively primitive culture of the Japanese.

More Syncretism

When one examines Shinto one finds therefore the result of another sycretistic process involving the fusion of elements from two or more religions to form a new religion. It should be noted that this type of syncretism was the unconscious variety, that is, it was not deliberately planned but more or less just happened as a result of gradual cultural interaction. In this case it was elements from the Chinese religions of Confucianism, Taoism, and Buddhism, the addition of which to some degree overwhelmed the naturism inherent in primitive Japanese religion. So overwhelmed were these native religious elements, in fact, that today little would be known of them were it not for a religious renaissance which took place in Japan in the Nineteenth Century under Emperor Meiji, who is often called the father of modern Japan. The Meiji reforms were intended to purge the new Japan of the effects of the influence of outside

"Izanagi and Izanami consulted together, saying 'We now have produced the Great-Eight-Island country, with the mountains, rivers, herbs, and trees. Why should we not produce someone who shall be lord of the universe?' They then together produced the Sun-Goddess, who was called Amaterasu-omi-kami."

—*The Nihongi*

77

nations, so that a purified and authentically Japanese culture might emerge. In this reform Shinto or Kami no Richi was reborn.

Primitive Japanese Religion

The earliest form of religion in Japan was most probably a kind of nature worship, centered on a sensitivity to the existence of divine spirits or kami especially present in nature. These spirits were the emanations of another whole order of existence, the world of the sacred. Primitive myths tell of the creation of the world in various ways. One story, probably originating in oral form before being written down in the Eighth Century in the *Kojiki* or Record of Ancient Matters and the *Nihongi* or Chronicles of Japan. In these two sacred texts one finds much of the creation myth in which the co-creators of the earth are at work. They are *Izanagi* and *Izanami,* the father and mother of creation. One day, the myth relates, Izanagi, seated on a cloud, took his spear and dipped it into the ocean, raising it high above the sky. As he did so, the drops of water fell back to the surface and formed the many hundreds of islands that make up Japan. This story is important inasmuch as it projects the belief in the divine origin and direct creation of the Japanese nation.

The Mikado

Another of the most important of these kami are the sun goddess, Amaterasu omi Kami and her consort, the moon god, Tsuki. It is the symbol of Amaterasu that appears on the nation's flag. The story of Amaterasu is important in tracing the divine origins of the imperial family. Her son married a human and by her fathered a demigod, half-man, half-god, named Jimmu Tenno. To him the Kami gave the throne of the island nation. Thus originated the belief in the divine descent of Japan's emperor or *mikado*. Up until the end of World War II, he was often referred to as the "son of heaven" or "heavenly king." This mythology was officially repromulgated by Emperor Meiji in his reforms. At the same time he reestablished what is called State Shinto as opposed to Sectarian Shinto. State Shinto existed primarily for the worship of the mikado, whereas Sectarian Shinto was for the worship of various kami.

This myth of the divine origins of the island-nation, along with the divinity of its emperor revived by Meiji, fueled a belief among the people and their leaders in a kind of "manifest destiny" of Japan, and led it into a policy of conquest and expansion throughout the Pacific Basin. It also explains the fanatical devotion to the mikado exemplified during World War II by the *kami-kaze* ("divine wind") pilots who committed ritual suicide in the act of flying their planes into American warships. State Shinto no longer exists in Japan, as the post-war reconstruction of Japan, under the supervision of the Supreme Command of Occupational Forces, outlawed the practice of emperor-worship. In 1946 Emperor Hirohito himself publicly renounced any claim to divinity in these words:

"The bonds between us and our countrymen...do not originate from mere myth and legend...They do not have their basis in the fictitious ideas that the emperor is manifest god and that the Japanese people are a race superior to other races and therefore are destined to rule the world..."

Needless to say, this caused great trauma to the people of Japan, a trauma which has almost destroyed the soul of that country. Today less than twenty-five percent of the Japanese identify themselves as religious in any way. Many of these have turned to various sects of Buddhism. Some, especially immediately following the War, became Christians. For others, materialism seems to have become their god. For the most part, it is the simple folk in rural areas who keep the old ways of Sectarian Shinto.

The Roots Of Shinto

As mentioned earlier, the classical form of Shinto relied on the three religions exported to Japan from China for much of its content. From Taoism came the confirmation of the native reverence for nature and its mystical powers. From Buddhism came several ideas. Since it was the mahayana tradition that was most popular in China, it was that form of Buddhism, which stressed the notion of the bodhisattvas or savior-gods, which was brought to Japan by Chinese merchants. This concept found a welcome home in a land fascinated by the kami and their comings and goings among the inhabitants of the earth. Shinto was also influenced to a degree by Buddhist ideas concerning the after-life, especially the mahayana belief in the "pure land of the buddhas," a place of endless bliss.

Influences On The Development Of Shinto	
Chinese Religion	**Its Principle Influence**
Taoism ————————→	Affirmation Of Nature Worship
Confucianism ————————→	Concern For Ethics And The Acquiring of Virtue
Manayana Buddhism ————————→	Multiple Deities And The Afterlife

It was Confucianism, however, that seemed to have the greatest impact on Shinto. Perhaps this was because its affirmation of class superiority and sanctioning of feudal social structures adapted well to the situation in Japan. At that time the emperor was ruler in name only. The country was actually controlled by numerous war-lords called *shoguns,* petty nobility who achieved and maintained their power through sheer strength of arms. Each war-lord was supported by a number of knights or *samurai* warriors. These warriors corresponded very closely to the medieval knights of feudal Europe, and conducted themselves according to similar high standards of chivalry and honor. This code of ethics by which the samurai lived and fought was called *bushido* or "the way of the fighting knight." Its rules included the samurai's willingness to lay down his life for the shogun, the expectation that he prefer death to dishonor, and that he even take his own life should it be necessary to save face. This ritual-suicide was called *hara-kiri* and may well have supplied the precedent for the kami-kaze flights of World War II. Samurai warriors were trained to show absolute respect for their masters and to all others in authority, to protect the weak, to come to the aid of those in need, and to be instruments of justice for those who had suffered wrong-doing.

Despite its waning popularity, Shinto remains an important part of Japanese culture. It is the undeniable source of countless customs and conventions among this people who have for so many centuries sought to follow "the way of the spirits."

Questions For Review

1. Explain the hybrid or syncretistic nature of the Shinto religion. How does it differ from the other syncretistic religion studied—the Sikhs?

2. Briefly describe the earliest form of Japanese religion. Which primitive elements of that remain part of Shinto today?

3. What impact did the so-called Meiji reforms of the Nineteenth Century have on the rebirth of Shinto?

4. What influence did Shinto have on the trend toward imperialism which saw Japan adopt the expansionist foreign policy which culminated in World War II?

5. Identify: Izanagi, Izanami, Amaterasu, Jimmu, Tenno, shogun, samurai, bushido, mikado, Kojiki, Nihongi, kami, hara-kiri, kami-kaze, Emperor Meiji, Emperor Hirohito, Sectarian Shinto, State Shinto.

Religions Of The Middle-East

"Hear with your ears that which is the sovereign good; with a clear mind look upon the two sides between which each man must choose for himself, watchful beforehand that the great test may be accomplished in our favor."

—*The Gathas*

81

Zoroastrianism

Of all the religions covered in this survey, Zoroastrianism is without a doubt the least significant numerically. Today there are fewer than 200,000 followers of this religion. It is not of interest because of its size, therefore, but rather because of the considerable influence it is believed to have exerted on the development of Judaism. Comparative religion scholars suggest that a number of concepts found in the Jewish faith were not original but had roots in the faith of this all but vanished religion from Persia.

Because of the ethnic nature of Judaism and its tradition of isolationism, remaining apart from and feeling superior to gentile religious groups, and even more importantly its concept of revelation, the idea of God communicating with his "chosen people" through the prophets and other inspired writers, it is often assumed that Judaism developed in a kind of theological vacuum. Scholars in recent years have come to believe otherwise. They theorize that during the period of the Babylonian Exile in the Sixth Century, B.C. the Jews had their eyes opened to a number of religious ideas not their own, and that this experience had a profound effect on the evolution of their own thinking. One of the sources of these foreign ideas may well have been the Zoroastrian faith which appears to have been widely known and discussed in Babylon by the time the exiles arrived. This much is known for a fact: the Jews returned from the Exile a different people than the one that entered it fifty years or so earlier. Once again, scholars see the possibilities of unconscious syncretism.

There is one more reason why scholars are so interested in this dwindling religious minority. Apparently there are two religions, not one, to be examined. The Zoroastrian faith was all but extinguished during the period of the Greek Empire created by Alexander the Great. Copies of its sacred book were ordered burned. Then, a century or so later the religion was revived, its sacred texts rewritten, pieced together from fragments of the original, leaving significant gaps and causing untold confusion but making for a fascinating study.

Zarathushtra Spitama

Persia, modern day Iran, at the time this religion orginated might be best described religiously as polytheistic, with temples erected in honor of hundreds of different deities, many of them associated with elements of nature. Astrology, the attempt to determine one's destiny through a reading of the alignment of the planets and stars, was very popular. The magi or wisemen of the Infancy Narrative in Saint Matthew's Gospel, described by the author as coming "from the East," were probably conceived as representatives of this tradition. The name Zoroaster is actually a Hellenization of the Persian *Zarathushtra*. Like so many other religious figures, much of what is known about Zarathushtra may lie more in the realm of legend than history.

Here is one version of his story. He is said to have been born sometime in the mid-Seventh Century, B.C. From his infancy it became apparent that he was destined to be a great religious leader. His mother experienced dreams in which not only his birth but the impact of his life was foretold. In addition, the king too was the recipient of dreams concerning Zarathushtra's birth, dreams which were interpreted by soothsayers as indicating in some way a threat to the king's absolute power over his subjects. For this reason the king ordered his ministers to seek out the child and put him to death. They had no choice but to obey, of course, but they were determined to eliminate the child in such a way that, if in fact the child was sent by the gods, they would not bring down the wrath of these gods on themselves.

These minions of the king first tried to put the child to death by offering him in sacrifice to Ahura Mazda, the fire-god, one of the many gods the Persians worshipped, feeling that Ahura would protect them should they incur the wrath of any other god in this act. They spirited the child away from his mother while she was preoccupied with other duties in the Spitama household. On discovering the child missing, she began to search frantically for him but to no avail. She decided to invoke the aid of one of her favorite gods, and so visited the temple of Ahura to pray. There she saw the infant standing upright in the brazier of the eternal fire kept burning in honor of the god by the temple priests. He seemed unscathed by the flames and, when beckoned, simply stepped out of the fire into his mother's waiting arms.

The next day the henchmen of the king once again kidnapped the child, this time bringing him out to a wide, green pasture where a herd of cattle were grazing peaceful-ly. They set the child down in the midst of the herd and then shouted and clapped their hands loudly to force the animals to stampede, and in so doing to crush the infant. The animals did begin to run wild, but the first cow to approach the child straddled him, protecting him with its own body as the others stampeded past. Once again the king's ministers were foiled. Zarathushtra's mother reclaimed her son unhurt for the second time.

The following day they tried one more time to fulfill the king's command to murder the child. This time, after stealing the infant once again, they brought him out to the wilderness and placed him in the den of a she-wolf who had just borne a litter of cubs. The mother was off hunting and these wicked men reasoned that when she returned she would kill the child and feed him to her cubs. This did not happen. On her return, the she-wolf, like that in the legend of Romulus and Remus, nursed the child with her own milk until its mother succeeded in finding him one last time.

Zarathushtra, The Religious Visionary

Nothing beyond this series of incredible stories is known about Zarathushtra until he had reached maturity and begun to preach his new religion. His ideas were quite different. He proclaimed Ahura Mazda as the one true God. As seen in the legend, this deity was worshipped by the Persians long before the time of Zarathushtra, but as one god among many gods, the god of light, symbolized by fire. All other gods, according to this new religion, were no longer to be considered gods, but to be acknowledged as pure spirits or angels who were in some way extensions of this one God. This angelic hierarchy—numbering 99,999—also included demons, chief of whom was Angra Mainyu, the prince of darkness.

Zarathushtra taught that each person has a body and a soul, and that the soul is im-mortal, living on after the body dies. He held that the soul is gifted by its creator with the ability to choose freely, and is in no way subject to destiny or fate. Each person lives but once and during that single lifetime must choose good and reject evil. Salva-tion is achieved through this moral struggle, and has nothing to do with the attainment of knowledge or enlightenment.

One of the most interesting features of Zarathushtra's new religion was his prophecy concerning the end of the world. He predicted that, three thousand years after his own death, Ahura Mazda would send a savior to preside over the fiery destruction of the world, a kind of Armageddon in which the angels of light would wage a final battle with and ultimately defeat the angels of darkness, inaugurating a golden age. This savior, named *Shaiyoshant,* would then judge the souls of all men and women who had ever lived, rewarding the good and punishing the wicked.

The Religion Spreads

Zarathushtra met with only limited success in developing a following for this new religion, beyond his own family and close friends, until, the story goes, the chief minister of the king saw his daughter one day and fell in love. He asked Zarathushtra for her hand in marriage, and of course he agreed. From that time on, Zarathushtra and his family became welcome in the highest social circles in Persia. Gradually he made converts from among this influential group, and before his death most upper class Persians had adopted the new faith as their own.

In the years that followed, a collection of sacred texts was made from what came to be known as the *Avesta*. The name comes from the name of the ancient Persian language in which it was first written. It consists of three parts. The *Yasna* is an anthology of sacred hymns and poems, including the *Gathas* which are believed to preserve some of the texts written by Zarathustra himself. The *Yashts* is another book of hymns, each of which is directed to the angels or spirits. Lastly, the *Vendidad* is a collection of mythology from earlier times, most probably reinterpreted through the vision of the Zoroastrian faith.

Its Influence On Judaism

As the Persian Empire began to expand, the influence of this new religion expanded with it, so that even before Cyrus had conquered Babylon in 539 B.C. it was known throughout the Middle-East. The time of Exile for the Jews, dating from the conquest of the Southern Kingdom and the subsequent destruction of its capitol, Jerusalem, in 587, until their liberation by Cyrus, in 538, marked a period of great change in Jewish thought. Exposed for the first time to many different religions and philosophies, the Jews certainly had ample opportunity to compare and reexamine many of their own religious ideas. It was, moreover, a time of intense introspection and reevaluation, as these exiles must have questioned why Yahweh had punished them in this way.

Prior to the Exile, less than one-third of the oral traditions of the Jews had been solidified in scripture. Unaware that they would be freed and allowed to return to Juda in less than fifty years, they probably decided to commit to writing much of their religious thinking in order to preserve the heritage for their children and grandchildren. By the time their Exile ended, the volume of written material, since accepted as part of the scriptural canon, had almost doubled. As they composed and edited, the scribes and other authors of scriptural works may have been inclined to draw on these extraneous religious ideas to express more perfectly their own thinking. Bible scholars, for example, have concluded that many of the religious stories found in the Hebrew Scriptures may have had their origins in non-Hebrew literature circulating in Sixth Century Babylon, a great crossroads of middle-eastern cultures.

Because of these many circumstances therefore, comparative religion scholars theorize that during the Exile Judaism was most susceptible to the influence of other religions, especially Zoroastrianism. Bible scholars, who can detect changes in language, vocabulary, and even grammatical construction, are able to distinguish, even within the same biblical book, parts that were written before the Exile from those written afterwards. Their studies show that many of the ideas that were assimilated by the Jewish tradition during that period were apparently unknown before that time. Though this theory cannot be absolutely proven, there does exist ample evidence that makes it probable.

Some of these new ideas, it is suggested, include the existence of the angels. In those parts of the Hebrew Scriptures undeniably composed prior to the Exile no angels are mentioned. In those composed later there are dozens of instances in which angels appear. The same conclusion is drawn with regard to Satan, the Prince of Darkness and the legions of devils. Satan does not appear in pre-Exilic texts. One might wonder about the story of the creation and fall of man presented in Genesis in which Satan plays a key role. Remember, though Genesis is placed as the first book in the Hebrew Scriptures, that does not mean that it was the first to be written. Biblical scholars contend that some sections of Genesis may have been among the last to be written. The whole notion of man's moral struggle to overcome evil, as his share in God's final victory over the forces of evil, expressed in the Genesis story of the fall of Adam and Eve is a theme that simply was not developed in Pre-Exilic material.

Still another group of ideas that appear in scripture only after the Exile concerns the end of the world. The concept of the messiah, which has become so integral to the Jewish faith, seems to have no precedent in pre-Exilic writing. Scholars wonder if the Zoroastrian idea of the Shaiyoshant could not be the inspiration for this hope among the Jews. Likewise the destruction of the world as we know it, with the subsequent judgment in which the good are rewarded and the evil punished, is a notion that appears to have been assimilated only after the Exile. Some scholars even go so far as to suggest that the notion of bodily resurrection, quite a late development in Judaism, may have had its roots in Zoroastrianism.

The Decline Of Zoroastrianism

The Persian Empire continued to dominate the Middle-East long after Cyrus ordered the Jews returned to Juda to rebuild their country. For over two hundred years they lived under Persian rule and influence. But by the middle of the Fourth Century, B.C., the Persian Empire was being threatened by a new power, that of Alexander the Great. It was Alexander who toppled the Persians and established what became known briefly as the Greek Empire. Although Alexander was not a Greek but a Macedonian, he favored the establishment of a Hellenic culture throughout his empire. The religion of the hated Persians was suppressed. Alexander ordered the public burning of every available text of the Avesta. Followers of Zoroastrianism were forced to worship the gods and goddesses of the Greek religion, and soon their religion had become a thing of the past.

This suppressed faith was not completely extinguished, however, and it enjoyed something of a rebirth in Persia in the late Third Century. Alexander had died young, without an heir, and so his empire was divided into three parts among his three strongest generals. In the part of the empire that included Persia a king named Artaxerxes founded a dynasty known as the Sassanian Dynasty. These kings tried to redefine the ethnic identity of Persians by resurrecting the old religion. They ordered that the Avesta be recomposed from fragments that had survived. Herein lies the second reason why comparative religion scholars are fascinated by Zoroastrianism.

A New Interpretation

In the reconstitution of the Avesta, written in the more modern language of Pahlavi, certain changes appear to have been made. Scholars are uncertain whether these changes came about as a result of the difficulty in translating the fragments which were written in Avesta, by this time a dead language, or whether scribes were simply reinterpreting the teachings of Zarathushtra through the prevailing philosophy of their day, Platonic Dualism. The once pure monotheism of Zarathushtra becomes an at best ambiguous form of dualism. Angra Mainyu, the leader of the angels of darkness, assumes what appears to be equality with Ahura Mazda. Scholars believe that this development or corruption may be attributed to the misinterpretation of a story found in the Vendidad which has Ahura Mazda fathering twin sons, one who chose good and the other evil. The story makes a point of the fact that the twin spirits were not created good or evil, but were created with the freedom to choose good or evil. The whole point of the story most probably was the doctrine of free will which formed an important part of Zarathustra's view of human nature. The story may have been misinterpreted under the strong influence of dualism to teach two supreme beings, one good and the other evil, which is the basis of dualistic religions.

The Parsis

Even if the Persians had not lost their power to the Greeks, it is unlikely they could have resisted the next onslaught of political and religious domination, that of the Moslems in the Seventh Century, A.D. Persia was one the first nations to fall to the expansion of the Arab Empire under the moslem caliphs. With the introduction of Islam in the year 637, Persians once again found themselves persecuted for their religious beliefs. Those who could afford to do so emigrated from Persia to the west coast of India and settled in the city of Bombay. There they were called "Parsis" which means "the Persians." Because of the Hindu caste system, along with the Indian tradition of religious tolerance, they have been able to maintain their ethnic and religious identity. Today almost ninety percent of all Zoroastrians in the world live not in Persia but in India. Those who remained in Persia have faced constant persecution under moslem rule, especially in recent years since the overthrow of the Shah and the establishment of Iran as an Islamic Republic.

Questions For Review

1. We are not interested in the Zoroastrian religion because it is large, but rather because it is important: it may have had a great influence on the development of Judaism. Explain this statement.

2. Why is it that comparative religion scholars are not sure whether the original religion founded by Zoroaster was monotheistic or dualistic?

3. What are some of the religious beliefs we associate so closely with Judaism which may well have originated in Zoroastrianism?

4. Just how did the Jews come under the influence of this religion, and what indications do we have that they may have adopted some of its ideas?

5. Why is such a sophisticated, well developed religion not embraced by more of the world's population? What historical circumstances altered its fate, where are most Zoroastrians located today, and finally, by what name are they more commonly known today?

6. Identify: Spitama, Ahura Mazda, Angra Mainyu, Avesta, shaiyotan, Parsi.

The Wailing Wall in old Jerusalem. "Never has the Divine Presence departed from the Western Wall." So says the Talmud.

Judaism

In the musical play, "Fiddler on the Roof," a story about a community of Russian Jews living in a town called Anatevka, the lead character named Tevye speaks this line: "Because of our tradition each one of us knows who he is, and what God expects of him." One will never fully understand the Jews until something is known of their tradition, the roots of this people of the land of Israel. Among all the religions of the world, the continuity of their tradition is indeed unique. The identity of each Jew is tied inextricably to the identity of the people and the land. Like Hinduism, Judaism derives its name from the land of its origins, and, like Hinduism also, it is an ethnic religion, as much a part of this people as the genes and chromosomes which make each of them unique. And this same tradition too places each Jew in a special relationship to the God who promised: "I will write my Law on your hearts...You shall be my people, and I will be your God" (Jeremiah 31:33).

The Patriarchs

The Jews trace the origins of their religion back to the Second Millenium, B.C. or B.C.E. ("before the common era," as the period is often referred to in Jewish histories). Around the year 1850 of this era, Yahweh revealed himself to a rich and powerful man named Abram, who owned thousands of sheep and goats and, for this reason, lived a nomadic existence, always on the move looking for fresh pasture for his flocks. God promised Abram that he would make him the father of a great nation, and for this reason he would no longer be Abram, but "Abraham," that is, "father of a multitude." There are two very important ideas to be noted here. One is that Abraham is not really the "founder" of Judaism. Rather God Himself is considered the founder; Abraham is merely the recipient of the revelation of God's plan for him and his descendants. The second point is the Promise itself. In making it, God established a special relationship with the Jewish People, a relationship that would endure for all time.

The covenant God made with Abraham was continued in his son Isaac and his grandson Jacob. As a sign of this covenant, Abraham was directed to circumcise each of his male descendants as well as every male member of his household. To this day circumcision is seen as the mark of every male Jew, and as the guarantee of his share in God's promise. To each of these descendants, as long as they honored Yahweh as their God, was promised a full and rich life. Jacob, also called "Israel," fathered twelve

"Yahweh said to Abram, 'Leave your country, your family, and your father's house, for the land I will show you. I will make you a great nation; I will bless you and make your name so famous that it will be used as a blessing. I will bless those who bless you: I will curse those who slight you. All the tribes of the earth shall bless themselves by you.'

—*Genesis 12:1-3*

89

sons who in turn are regarded as the founders of the Twelve Tribes of Israel. This is the family tree of the Hebrew People. The oral tradition of stories concerning these ancestors orginated long before the Book of Genesis, which puts them into writing, began to take shape.

The People Become A Nation

"When Israel came out of Egypt,
the House of Jacob from a foreign nation,
Judah became his sanctuary
and Israel his domain..." (Psalm 114)

Genesis concludes with the passing of the last of Jacob's sons, all of whom died in Egypt where they had sought relief from an extended drought in Canaan where they were living with their flocks. Here in the Land of the Nile is where the Book of Exodus begins, a book so named because of its central event, occurring in the year 1290, God's deliverance of His People from bondage to the Egyptians, their subsequent departure from Egypt, and their journey to the land that God was to give them, the Promised Land.

Under the leadership of a man called Moses of the Tribe of Levi, the Hebrews followed God's directions to establish themselves in a new land, a land "flowing with milk and honey." If Abraham is acknowledged as the father of the Jewish People, then Moses may be regarded as the father of the Nation. It was to Moses on Mount Sinai that God revealed His Law expressed in the Ten Commandments. It was Moses who unified the twelve tribes into one people, one nation. Under Moses too came the further codification of laws by which this people would live.

When the Hebrews took possession of the Promised Land, they divided it up among the tribes, each tribe being ruled by a chief or "judge." For this reason this period of Jewish history is called the Age of the Judges, lasting from about the year 1250 to about 1000. "Judges" were more than just tribal leaders; they also were the religious lights of their people. In addition to these judges, there were also various prophets who usually saw their role as one of chiding their people to observe God's laws more generously. During this period the Hebrews were almost constantly at war with their neighbors, tribes and peoples from whom they had wrested their new land. Toward the end of this period, they began to realize that the independence of the twelve tribes was frequently a costly disadvantage, particularly when fighting against a stonger and more unified enemy. And so they decided to ask the prophet Samuel to choose a king for them.

The Monarchy

Samuel annointed Saul the first King of Israel. He had a difficult challenge—to unify a people earlier divided by tribal loyalties. It was a challenge that was not entirely met until the second king, who was David. Under King David Jerusalem became the capitol, and thus began an institution that would become part of the very essence of Judaism, namely the centrality of the city of Jerusalem to the identity of every Jew. "If I forget you, Jerusalem, may my right hand wither" (Psalm 137). In order to give the Hebrews a sense of national identity, scholars suggest, David inaugurated the "pilgrim festivals." These were religious festivals for which elaborate rituals were staged at the Capitol. (Probably one of these celebrations was the occasion of Jesus' trimphal entry into Jerusalem which is commemorated by Christians on Palm Sunday.) Every Hebrew male was obligated to come to at least one each year. Seeing the King's palace and the other magnificent public buildings that David was erecting there helped to instill a sense of patriotism in his people. Soon the nation began to be solidified. It prevailed against its enemies and even exacted tribute from its weaker neighbors. Scripture scholars believe that his reign saw the beginnings of the literary tradition of Scripture. The reign of David is generally regarded as the highpoint of the monarchy period of Jewish history.

Star of David

David was succeeded by one of his many sons, Solomon. Under his rule Israel prospered and grew even stronger, rivaling even the great kingdom of Egypt. It was Solomon who built the First Temple at Jerusalem. This accomplishment was a milestone in the evolution of the way Hebrews worshipped their God. With this development the religious leadership of Israel shifted from the charismatic and often anti-establishment style of the prophets to the more stable and highly organized system of temple priesthood. With the institution of monarchial rule and the establishment of a temple priesthood, the Hebrews were becoming more and more like their neighbors. This was true in other ways as well.

Solomon was a wise and generous king, but he had one fatal flaw. His weakness was women. Like other kings in the middle-east at the time he had a harem. The Bible records that he had over three hundred wives, many of them foreign. Some of these persuaded him to build for them temples to their own deities, and thus Jerusalem by the end of his reign was crowded with temples to foreign gods. Many Hebrews participated in these religions and in so doing broke the covenant made by their ancestors almost a thousand years earlier: the promise to worship only Yahweh.

At the death of Solomon his son Rehoboam succeeded to the throne. He was faced with a large debt incurred by the endless building programs his father had carried on. When his subjects asked for some tax relief, Rehoboam refused to grant their request. At this, civil war broke out with all but the tribe of Juda, David's own tribe, and that of Benjamin revolting. There were led by Jeroboam who had served in Solomon's army. Jereboam was crowned King of Israel, which included the remaining tribes, and established what is sometimes called the Northern Kingdom. He ordered that a temple for worship be set up at Bethel in the North and forbade his subjects to go up to Jerusalem. Rehoboam was strong enough to remain King of Juda, or the Southern Kingdom, and worship continued to be offered to Yahweh at the temple of Jerusalem, but Rehoboam and his successors continued to allow as well the worship of other gods. This marked the beginning of the Divided Kingdom period.

Now divided and weakened, it was only a matter of time when stronger neighbors would reassert themselves. Israel was the first to fall, when in 722 the Kingdom of Assyria conquered it, scattering the northern tribes. Juda was eventually forced to pay tribute. During this period the prophetic tradition was revived, and several of the greatest prophets appeared, men like Isaiah and Jeremiah. Their principal concern was the condemnation of the worship of false gods, by then common in the North as well as the South. They tried to convince their countrymen that the reason Israel's power had been eclipsed by other nations was their failure to observe the Covenant. Frequently they likened the Hebrews' idolatry to the infidelity of an adulterous spouse. They longed for a return to the golden days of the Davidic Monarchy, a time when Israel was one—one in political unity, and one in faith in the God who had brought them out of Egypt.

Ancient Palestine, 800 B.C.E.

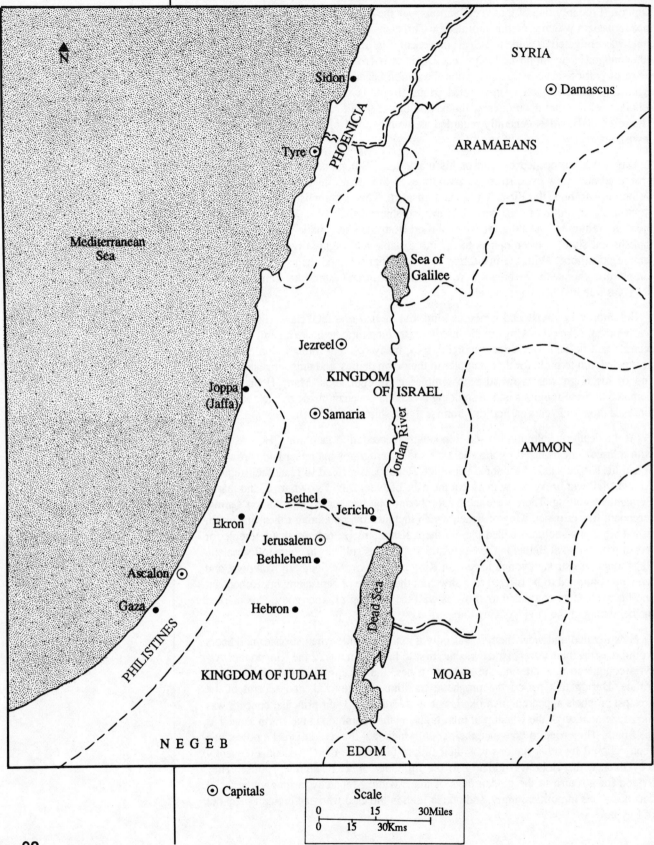

N

SYRIA

Sidon •

⊙ Damascus

PHOENICIA

ARAMAEANS

Tyre ⊙

Mediterranean
Sea

Sea of
Galilee

Jezreel ⊙

KINGDOM
OF ISRAEL

Joppa
(Jaffa) •

Jordan River

⊙ Samaria

AMMON

Bethel •

Jericho •

Ekron •

Jerusalem ⊙

Bethlehem •

Ascalon ⊙

Dead Sea

Gaza •

PHILISTINES

Hebron •

KINGDOM OF JUDAH

MOAB

N E G E B

EDOM

⊙ Capitals

Scale

0   15   30Miles

0   15   30Kms

The Babylonian Exile

The Assyrian Empire was soon succeeded by the Babylonians. Shortly thereafter, Nebuchadnezzar conquered the Southern Kingdom, destroying the Solomonic Temple and most of the rest of Jerusalem. In the year 587 he exiled all of its leading citizens to his capitol at Babylon. Priests, lawyers, members of the nobility, wealthy merchants and landowners—all were uprooted from their homes and forced to move together with their families. Most probably his intention was to leave the remaining populace without leadership, thereby insuring easy control of the subjugated lands. The same ploy was used more than once in modern times by the Soviets. In 1940 in the Baltic States of Lithuania, Latvia, and Estonia those leaders of society who were not executed for actively opposing sovietization were exiled to Siberia when those countries were annexed to the U.S.S.R.

The period of the Exile, which lasted almost a half-century, was a time of great change for these Judeans or "Jews." As mentioned in the section on the Zoroastrians, it was a time for theological reflection and agonizing re-appraisal of their tradition. As with a person convicted of crimes and sent off to prison, the Jews reflected on their predicament. Where had they gone wrong? How had they so offended their God, that he would punish them so harshly? How had they violated the covenant He had established with their ancestors?

In many ways the Exile constituted a major turning-point in their history, just as the Exodus had. Fearing that their children and grandchildren would not be able to appreciate their magnificent and unique heritage, they began to commit many of their oral traditions to writing, almost doubling the body of Hebrew Scriptures begun during the first stages of the monarchy. Without a Temple in which to offer sacrifice, they instituted synagogue worship, an unbloody sacrifice of praise and thanksgiving drawn largely from their expanding scriptures. This liturgical form was retained even after the Jews returned to Jerusalem, so that by the time of Christ every community of Jews, no matter how small, had its synagogue for daily prayer. The absence of temple-worship also affected the religious leadership. Priestly influence gave way to rabbinical authority. Rabbis, who were trained in the *Torah* or Law, led these synagogue services and instructed others in the observance of the Law. Even the practice of keeping the Sabbath holy may not have become firmly established until the Exile.

Doctrinally, the Jews appear to have progressed from monolatry, or the acceptance of the existence of many gods, but the worship of only one, to a pure monotheism, the denial of any gods other than the One God, Yahweh. "Hear, O Israel, the Lord your God is one" (Duet 6:4), the often recited *Shema Yisrael* prayer. The Psalms offer a good reflection of this transition. In Psalm 95, one written prior to the Exile and obviously monolatrous, the psalmist sings: "For Yahweh is a great God, a greater king than all other gods..." But in Psalm 115 and again in Psalm 135, which incidentally is used regularly in the synagogue service even today, both of which were probably written either during or shortly after the Exile, one hears this triumphant statement of pure monotheism:

> Pagan idols are silver and gold, the work of human hands: they have mouths, but they cannot speak, eyes, but they cannot see, ears, but they cannot hear, and not a breath in their mouths. Their makers will end up like them, and so will anyone who trusts in them (Psalm 135:15-18).

During their Exile the Jews began to identify idolatry as a major cause of their downfall. Sections of the Hebrew Scriptures identified with this period are rife with instances of this rejection of idolatry. Not only did they condemn the worship of false gods, but they even developed the notion that the polygamy of Solomon, with his subsequent building of shrines and temples to the foreign gods of his many wives, must likewise be condemned. Monogamy became the rule rather than the exception, and divorce was permitted only for good reason. At the same time, a trend toward misogynism, or prejudice against women in general, begins to appear. Adam's laying the blame for his disobedience to God at the feet of Eve in the Story of the Fall in the third chapter of Genesis is a good example of this very negative and sexist attitude.

The longer the Jews endured their Exile, the stronger the yearning to return to their homeland grew. It is no wonder then that this intense longing spawned the hopes of deliverance. Just as Yahweh had freed their ancestors from the bondage of the Egyptians, they began to nourish the hope that He would relent and restore their fortunes once again. One is reminded of this sentiment in "Fiddler" when, as the Jews of Anatevka are ordered to move from their homes to be relocated, Tevye tearfully asks: "Wouldn't this be a good time for the Messiah to come?" Before their Exile, the Jews don't seem to have any such hopes, but the multitude of allusions to a Messiah found in post-exilic passages of the Scriptures seem to indicate that this concept had become firmly entrenched during that time.

Development Of Jewish Thought	
Before The Exile	After The Exile
About one-third of the Scriptures composed	Almost three-fourths of the Scriptures complete
Temple Worship only	Synagogue Worship common
Little evidence for Sabbath Observance	Sabbath Observance has become a hallmark of Judaism
Monolatrous Monotheism	Strict Monotheism
Few Messianic ideas	Messianism is dominant
After-Life unclear	After-Life includes the resurrection
No mention of angels	Angels and devils
Doctrinal Unity	Sectarianism
Jews all live in Israel	Many Jews in *Diaspora*
Polygamy common	Strictly Monogamous
Prophets and Priests provide leadership	Rabbinical Leadership

Still another change in Jewish life is attributable to the exilic experience, and that is what is known as the *diaspora* or the existence of Jews living outside of Israel. When the Jews were finally liberated by Cyrus, King of Persia, in the year 539, many Jews freely chose to remain in Babylon and did not return with the others. This began the custom of Jews living in other parts of the Mediterranean World. It was to these "expatriate Jews" of the diaspora or dispersion that Saint Paul first preached the Gospel.

Finally, as so often happens among religious groups when changes occur, after the Exile Jews were never again to be doctrinally united. Many could not or would not accept the changes. This resulted in what is known as "sectarian Judaism." By the time of Christ there were many different sects of Jews. In the Gospels, for example, one finds references to Pharisees, Sadducees, and even Zealots. These groups all had their own ideas. The Sadducees, for example, would not accept any of the additions to the first five books in the Scriptures: to them, only the Torah contained God's word. Nor would they accept the belief in the messiah or the reign of God he would establish on earth, with its accompanying notion of an after-life: to them life ended at the grave.

Return From Exile

For the next two centuries the Jews lived under Persian rule. They were allowed a certain amount of autonomy, especially in religious matters. The first major undertaking, in fact, was to begin the process of rebuilding the temple. Though sacrifices could now be made to Yahweh once more, the "spiritual sacrifice" of praise and thanksgiving in the synagogue service was continued. As directed by Cyrus, the Jews made an effort to recover what they could of their previous material prosperity and cultural life. During this period a group of leading citizens met regularly to discuss important issues of the remnant community which had returned from Babylon. Initially it was made up of priests and levites together with the heads of the most important families. This group eventually evolved into what was known by the time of Christ as the Sanhedrin.

By the middle of the Fourth Century, B.C., the Persian Empire was on the wane, and the Greeks were beginning to assert themselves. Alexander the Great, son of King Philip of Macedonia, defeated the Persians and established his own empire, stretching from Greece all the way to India. Alexander's moment in the sun, however, was short-lived: he died heirless at the age of thirty-four. The empire was divided up among his top three generals, with that part which included Israel coming under one and then another's successors for the next hundred years or so. Finally the Seleucids who made Damascus in Syria their capitol took control. The Jews lived under this Syrian domination for another thirty years.

Independence

In the year 165, a Syrian King named Antiochus Epiphanes IV decided to enforce the Hellenization of Jewish culture, including religion. He ordered that statues of the Greek gods and goddesses be placed in the temple and that the Jews be pressed to offer them worship. The Jews, who had suffered greatly under various rulers since the Exile, vehemently resisted. A rebellion led by Mattathias, a priest, and his son Judas Maccabeus broke out, and after two long years of fighting, the Syrians were finally driven out of the country, and Israel was declared an independent nation once again. When the Jews reentered their temple, they had to rededicate it to Yahweh, the only true God. This event is commemorated each year by Jews in the Channukah festival. The Jews ruled themselves by means of the Sanhedrin, with the high priest acting as a kind of moderator, thus forming what ammounted to theocratic rule.

With the reassertion of priestly power a new emphasis was placed on temple sacrifice. In addition, because of the real power which the priests enjoyed, the corruption which almost inevitably followed created still another faction. Many who, like the Prophet Amos, were appalled at the externalism of temple sacrifices, who favored the "spiritual worship" of the synagogue service, and who had great expectations for the coming of a messiah, rebelled against priestly control of religious matters and moved out to the desert, establishing themselves at Qumran on the northwest shore of the Dead Sea. These were the Essenes, a kind of monastic community which produced what are known today as the "Dead Sea Scrolls."

For one hundred years the Jews enjoyed relative freedom and independence, though they were never entirely free from outside threats. In 63, Pompei marched into Jerusalem and declared Israel a Roman province. Independence was lost. Rome agreed to allow the Sanhedrin to meet to handle purely religious matters; all other decisions were made by a Roman procurator or governor. Eventually the half-Jewish, half-Arab Herod was made a puppet-king and given limited powers to govern some parts of Israel. It was this Herod who built what is sometimes referred to as the Second Temple. Built on the exact site of the one built by Solomon, the Herodian Temple was better than twice the size of the original. It was the same great builder, Herod the Great, who designed and completed the fortress at Masada on the shores of the Dead Sea, not far from Qumran. At the turn of the Christian era, Herod's descendants were still in power.

Jewish History In The Christian Era

The first significant date in Jewish history in the Christian Era is the year 70, for that marks the Roman seige of Jerusalem and the destruction of the Second Temple. Shortly after the death of Jesus, unrest was common in Jerusalem and throughout Israel, stirred up by numerous revolutionaries, some even claiming to be the Messiah, who were for driving the Romans into the sea and declaring independence. The Romans, who realized they must send a message to their other provinces, were determined to put down any insurrection which might develop. They mobilized legions from all over the Empire, mounted an enormous attack, and in the end laid waste to the Capitol itself.

The last of these patriots, numbering over nine hundred, escaped to Herod's old fortress at Masada and held out there for over two years. Finally, the Romans took Masada too by building an earthen ramp against the almost impregnable mountain bastion. The Jewish historian Josephus provides a complete account of the seige. When the Roman general, Silva, entered the fortress, he discovered every last Jew already dead. These patriots had entered a death pact with one another: lots had been drawn, and one man in every ten was chosen to kill the rest, then more lots and more killing until only one remained, who then took his own life—a final act of defiance against the Romans.

After the destruction of Jerusalem, the vast majority of Jews living in Juda fled. Many left Israel altogether, moving on to join relatives living in the Diaspora in other parts of the Mediterranean World; others moved north into the Gallilee, and some of these staged further rebellions, the last in the year 135. None of them succeeded. This people, to whom Yahweh had given this land as their home, were now without a homeland. For a long time Jews were welcome in other parts of the Empire. Most of them were literate and had skills and crafts with which they could support themselves. But always, and wherever they went, they looked back to their homeland, hoping one day to return.

In the year 313, the Emporer Constantine issued the Edict of Milan, a decree which ended the persecution of Christianity and paved the way for its establishment as the state religion. This in fact did occur with one of Constantine's successors, when in the year 389 Emperor Theodosius decreed that all non-Christian religions were to be proscribed. Judaism was excepted, perhaps because of its affinity to Christianity, but it was now a tiny island in a great sea of Christianity.

The next development which had significant impact on the Jews was the birth of Islam in Arabia in the Seventh Century. Within a hundred years Islam had spread throughout the Middle-East. At first Jews were respected as "people of the Book," in recognition of the two religions' common belief in one God, not to mention the Moslems' tracing their religious heritage back to the Patriarch Abraham. There was a large and prosperous Jewish population in Babylon dating from the time of the Exile. Jews there enjoyed a kind of golden age during the Ninth and Tenth Centuries especially, producing great philosophers and scientists as well as an immense body of rabbinical scholarship including commentaries on the Torah called the *Talmud*. Unfortunately, the larger the Arab Empire became, the less tolerant it became of "infidels." By the turn of the first millennium of the Christian Era, most Jews were once again on the move, this time further west, joining large numbers of their fellow countrymen living in Western Europe.

At this time Europe was still very much in the grips of the Dark Ages, and so the skills and education of most of the Jews arriving found a welcome home there. This hospitality was not to last forever. It was not long before Christians from the West attempting to make pilgrimages to the Holy Land were met with hostility and aggression from the Arab World. Soon religious wars or crusades were being fought to secure their right to visit the holy places. Europeans who returned from the crusades brought back with them a fear and hatred of non-Christians which was transferred to the Jews living among them at home. About the same time, the inquisitions were inaugurated in order to root out heresies and challenges to the Catholic Faith. Naturally the Jews suffered from this development as well as heretical Christians. Many Jews had no choice but to "convert" to Christianity if they wished to preserve their rights and sometimes their lives. There is some evidence, however, that indicates many of these converts continued to practice their religion secretly.

By the year 1300 Jews were expelled from England; by 1400 from France; and by 1500 from Spain. Shakespeare's "Merchant of Venice" with its parody of the Jewish money lender, Shylock, provides a good insight into the antisemitism which abounded in Europe during the Middle Ages. Because of this change in the acceptance of Jews in Western Europe, another migration began, this time to the still undeveloped nations of Eastern Europe, countries like Poland, the Slavic nations, and Russia. For the same reasons that they were once welcome in Western Europe, Jews found their skills and talents very much in demand in Eastern Europe.

Orthodox Jewish youth engrossed in prayer at Jerusalem's Wailing Wall on the eve of Yom Kippur, the Day of Atonement. The solemn observance is a time for prayer, fasting and a reappraisal of the past for all those of the Hebrew faith.

There was a large concentration of Jews living in Eastern Europe at the beginning of the Eighteenth Century. By the end of that century, governments of those countries were passing discriminatory laws against Jews, limiting their rights and in many cases denying them full citizenship. This situation determined two of the most significant developments in modern Jewish history. One development was a massive migration to America, where they could find religious freedom and full citizenship. The second concerned those left behind, who suffered through that horrendous genocidal experience known as the Holocaust.

In 1933 when Adolf Hitler took power in Germany and established the Third Reich there were approximately sixteen million Jews in the world. By the end of World War II that number had diminished to about ten million. In the space of twelve years, six million Jews had been put to death. The Holocaust had little to do with religion, but rather was an attempt by the Nazi government of Germany to eliminate this foreign ethnic stock from among its subjects. This same "solution" was employed to rid Europe of its gypsy populations, and in fact hundreds of thousands of them were also put to death. It is not unimportant to recall that hundreds of millions of dollars worth of property confiscated in this genocidal persecution went directly to the government. Whatever the psychotic reasoning was, this experience has left a scar on the Jewish world community that may never heal.

The State Of Israel

By far the single most important event in modern Jewish history has been the establishment of the modern State of Israel. Beginning with the exodus from Eastern Europe at the end of the Nineteenth Century, many Jews had been returning to Palestine, then part of the Ottoman Empire. This movement continued and even increased at the end of World War I when Palestine became a British protectorate. Though such immigration was severely limited, Jews continued to arrive by the thousands each month, many of them illegally. The British were concerned with the effect such an influx would have on the Arab population. Nevertheless, the British government was determined to provide some solution to this desire of Jews to return to their homeland. In 1917 Parliament passed the Balfour Declaration which promised to create an independent state for the immigrants some time in the future.

Jews themselves were actively working towards this end. The Zionist movement founded by Theodor Herzl at the beginning of the Twentieth Century was active in pursuing the dream of reestablishing a homeland. This movement lobbied governments to gather support for a Jewish state and encouraged Jews to emigrate to Palestine to establish a presence there. Jews from all over the world, but especially from Eastern Europe, did return. This return to Israel was called *aliyah*. These determined and talented immigrants were soon working miracles, turning pieces of unwanted desert into productive farms.

In the years immediately following World War II the effort picked up momentum. The United Nations established a commission to study the possibilities, and world opinion seemed in favor of a Jewish state, perhaps feeling that this might in some small way compensate for the unspeakable tragedy of the Holocaust. Even before the United Nations had acted on May 14, 1948 the Jews of Palestine decided to declare an independent State of Israel, organized around a provisional cabinet headed by David ben

Gurion as its first prime minister. Within twenty-four hours the United States had recognized the new nation.

Sectarian Judaism

It is probably safe to say that since the Exile Jews have been divided into sects or factions. This was true at the time of Christ, when specific sects of Jews are mentioned in the Gospels. It is true today. Ethnically even there is some difference among the world's Jewish population. Since the time that the Jews ceased to be a nation and became a people who live in many other nations, Jews are now able to distinguish among themselves two principal groups. *Ashkenazim* is Hebrew for "Germans" and is used to designate Jews originating not only in Germany but anywhere in Eastern Europe, while *Sephardim,* the Hebrew for "Spaniards," is the name given to Jews who, after their expulsion from Spain, moved to North Africa and parts of the Middle-East. Each of these ethnic groups have their own traditions, dialects, and ritual practices. Sephardic Jews tend to be less well educated than Ashkenazic Jews. The language called *Yiddish,* commonly used by Ashkenazic Jews is actually a combination of a German dialect with Hebrew, and written in Hebrew characters. Gradually these differences are fading, of course, but they still exist to some degree.

The religious differences among Jews are more significant. There are today five principal interpretations of Judaism. Three of them are well known: the Orthodox, the Conservative, and the Reform traditions. Two others, more recent, are less known outside the Jewish community itself: the Humanist and the Reconstruction groups. The differences among Orthodox, Conservative, and Reform Jews arise basically from a different view of the Law, how it ought to be observed, and what if any accommodations might be made to the modern age. Humanist or Naturalist Judaism together with Reconstructionism are totally new approaches to Jewish tradition, both of which hold that revelation is completely relative making no absolute demands in terms of the way one responds to God. Most mainstream Jews are convinced that these modern approaches are without biblical justification and therefore have no right to identify themselves as Jewish.

Of all the world's Jews more than half are Orthodox. These Jews believe that the Law is central, and its observance must be unconditional. They follow 613 laws found in the Torah, and interpreted down through history by rabbinical authorities. Orthodox Judaism, because of its slavish observances, is often accused of being caught up in literalism, the letter of the law rather than its spirit. It is a very demanding tradition. Adult males are expected to attend daily synagogue services if at all possible, and if not to recite daily prayers at home. The liturgy in orthodox synagogues is conducted in Hebrew. For this reason, young boys attend Hebrew school after regular school several days each week in order to achieve a proficiency in the language. Orthodox men always keep their heads covered, frequently with a small skull-cap called a *yarmulke,* wear beards, and practice the strictest modesty, never exposing arms or legs. When praying the *tallit* or prayer shawl is worn over the head and shoulders together with the *tefillin* or phyllacteries, small leather cases containing parchment on which passages of the Scriptures are written, bound around the arm with leather straps.

The sabbath or *shabbat,* which begins at sunset on Friday and ends at sunset on Saturday, is kept according to rigid guidelines, with no work whatsoever permitted: even the preparation of food is forbidden, so that the sabbath meal must be prepared

before sunset on Friday. They keep strict dietary laws, completely abstaining from certain foods and not mixing others together. Food must be prepared according to special rules and regulations. This observance is called *kashruth* or the laws of kosher foods. For example, orthodox do not eat any pork products, nor do they eat shellfish of any type, perhaps because both of these animals are scavengers. Nor do they eat meat products on the same plate as dairy products. Separate sets of dishes are required, and they must be washed separately as well. Because the Law itself is seen as unchanging, their observance of the Law does not change either. To see an Orthodox Jew in the Twentieth Century is to see one in the Tenth Century. For this reason, Orthodox Judaism is still very patriarchal. Women do not sit with the men in the synagogues but are seated at the back or in the balcony. Orthodox Jews do not enter mixed marriages: they marry only other Orthodox, and not to do so would be to abandon one's Faith.

Among Orthodox Jews there are some extremists or "Ultra-Orthodox," as they are sometimes called. One such group is the Hasidic sect. These Jews set themselves apart from mainstream Judaism completely, even to the point of opposing Zionism and the establishment of the State of Israel: they look forward to the spiritual reign of the Messiah instead. Assimilation to a more modern, pluralistic society is the last thing they want. Many Jews themselves are critical of these ultra-orthodox, seeing their clinging to a style of dress and grooming as throwbacks to a medieval Eastern European Jewish culture that time has passed by.

Reform Judaism began at the beginning of the Nineteenth Century as a movement among European Jews who were growing more and more prosperous, and who for many reasons desired to become assimilated to the cultures native to the countries in which they were living. The religious faith that they professed was so foreign to those populations that it made the Jews more conspicuous than they would like. They attempted to accommodate their religious laws and customs to what was considered simply a change in their circumstances. They adapted their religious faith to the modern world, a world which was by and large not Jewish. Reform Jews abandoned the use of Hebrew in their services, adopting in its place the vernacular. Unlike the orthodox, musical instruments may be used to accompany congregational singing. They limit synagogue attendance to the sabbath and the holy days: there are no daily services. Seating in the synagogue is mixed: families sit together. Today there are women rabbis. In addition to the *bar-mitzvah* or confirmation rite for boys, they have added a *bat-mitzvah* for girls. Dietary regulations are generally considered to be no longer relevant.

The Three Most Popular Forms Of Judaism Today

Orthodox	Reform	Conservative
The Largest	The Smallest	In the Middle
Observance of the Law	Disregard for Legalism	Partial Observance
Strict Dietary Rules	No Concern for Diet	Some Dietary Rules
Strict Dress Code	No Dress Code	Dress for Worship
Daily Liturgy	Weekly Liturgy	Weekly Liturgy
Hebrew in Liturgy	Some Hebrew Used	Some Hebrew Used
Patriarchal	Women Participate Fully	Less Patriarchal

Conservative Judaism represents a middle ground between Orthodox and Reform Judaism. The movement dates from around the middle of the Nineteenth Century, and developed likewise primarily in Germany. Many Jews at this time felt that Reform Judaism went too far. They too felt the need to adapt to a more modern age, but were unwilling to do so at the cost of abandoning their traditions totally. There was therefore a conscious effort to "conserve" much that is unique in Judaism while at the same time modifying observance of the Law. Not only Hebrew but also the vernacular is used at the weekly synagogue service. Conservative Jewish men wear the yarmulke and the tallit, but normally only in the synagogue. Some dietary laws are still observed, but customs such as separate sets of dishes for the different food groups are not adhered to strictly. After many years of resisting the innovation, Conservative Jewish congregations now ordain women to the rabbinate. Unlike the majority of Orthodox Jews, Conservative and Reform Jews have moved away from the expectation of a personal messiah. Instead they look forward to the time when peace and justice rule, and Jews are reinstated as the "light of all nations." Many see the erection of the State of Israel as the beginning of this golden age.

The Jewish Festivals

There are several important festivals in Judaism, but none more important than the "High Holy Days" of *Rosh Hashanah* and *Yom Kippur*. The Jewish New Year or feast of Rosh Hashanah occurs in September or October in the western calendar. The Jewish liturgical calendar is based on a lunar calendar of ten months, and for this reason it does not occur on the same day of the same month each year. It is an autumn festival, reflecting the agricultural economy of early Judaism. The day itself is signaled in by the sounding of the *shofar* or ram's horn. On the tenth day of this new year's festival, Yom Kippur or the Day of Atonement is celebrated. This day is kept as a fast day, and no food is taken until sunset when the fast is broken with a joyous feast. The day itself is dedicated to prayer in the synagogue and atonement for past sins.

Perhaps the best known of all the Jewish festivals is that of the Passover. It is celebrated according to a uniform ritual called a *seder* which revolves around the eating of a special family meal, presided over by the head of the household. It commemorates the Exodus of the Jews from bondage to the Egyptians. This feast is actually the result of the fusion of two different rites developed separately. The Hebrew word for this festival is *pesach,* a word which refers to the offering of the first lambs born to the flocks of sheep kept by early Jewish shepherds. This lamb was offered to Yahweh in gratitude for the fertility of the flock, and in the hope that many others would be born as well so that the flocks would multiply. This festival was later merged with that of *massoth,* a feast which was likewise celebrated long before the Exodus. Massoth was a feast of first fruits offered by farmers, who took the very first sheaves of wheat to appear on the spring wheat, and made from them an unleavened bread without any yeast which was then offered to Yahweh. These two agrarian feasts were combined and given a new significance, that of the commemoration of the historical event of the Exodus. It was at a celebration of the Passover that Jesus instituted the Eucharist, giving the Jewish ritual new meaning.

Two additional agrarian feasts in the calendar were also given an historical significance. They are *Shavouth* and *Succoth*, the spring and autumn harvest festivals respectively. To Shavouth which occurs in May or June was attached the historical commemoration of the giving of the Torah on Mount Sinai, and so it is sometimes

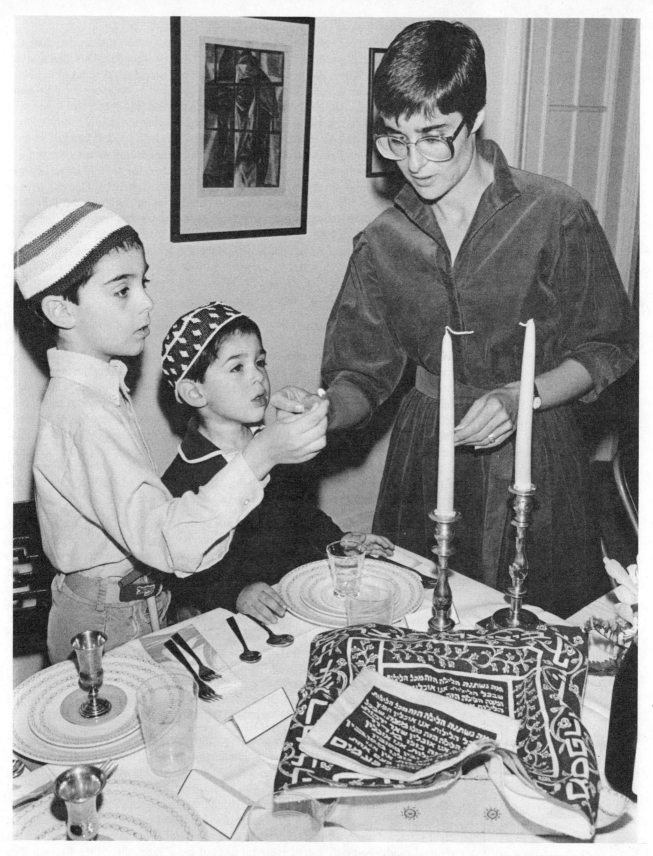

The lighting of the candles begins the Passover celebration.

referred to as the Feast of Tablets. This feast was kept on the fiftieth day after the second day of Passover at which time offerings of wheat were made. This then was the day of Pentecost (fiftieth day) on which Christians celebrated the descent of the Holy Spirit on the apostles gathered in the upper room. To Succoth which occurs in September or October was attached the historical commemoration of the Jews living a nomadic existence for forty years in the Sinai before entering the Promised Land. They were reminded of this part of their history because during this period farmers, usually with their whole families, moved right out into the fields, living in tents to take advantage of the light in order to complete the harvest before the autumn rains. For this reason it is sometimes referred to as the Feast of Tabernacles or Tents. One unique feature of this festival was a procession from the outskirts of the city into the Temple at Jersalem, a procession in which palm fronds and willow branches were used. Scripture scholars believe that this may have been the occasion of Jesus' triumphal entry into the city, and that the evangelists may have placed the incident in the spring shortly before the Passion simply to highlight the contrast in attitudes among the fickle crowds. These two feasts, therefore, like Pesach and Massoth, are probably very ancient, celebrated even before the time of the Exodus.

There are two other major festivals in the Hebrew calendar, *Purim* or the Feast of Lots and *Channukah* or the Feast of Lights. Both are feasts which commemorate events from Jewish history in which the Jewish people were delivered from adversity. Purim celebrates an event in the Fourth Century which is recorded in the Book of Esther. A Jewess named Esther had been wed to the Persian King Ahasueros. The king's minister, a man named Haman, had hatched a plot to kill the Jews and had cast lots to determine the best day on which to carry out his plan of destruction. Mordecai, one of the leaders of the Jewish community, discovered Haman's plan and begged Queen Esther to intercede with Ahasueros. The King was moved by Esther and ordered Haman executed instead. Thus Esther became a heroine to her people. Scholars question the historicity of this event. The fictitious King Ahasueros might be either Xerxes I or Artaxeres II, but there is no record of such a plot in Persian histories.

There are two possible explanations for the story found in the Book of Esther. One suggests the story is an attempt to counter a misogynistic attitude that spread through the Jewish community after the Exile, which was alluded to in the section concerning the transition in Jewish thought during and after the Exile. Another theory documents a Babylonian feast of lots celebrated there at the same time of the year, in February or March. Apparently during the Exile some Jews participated in this feast which was often characterized by raucous behavior, and in fact some continued to observe it even after the Exile. Purim, this second explanation reasons, may have been instituted to supplant this pagan debauchery. One wonders which came first: the story of Esther or the feast of lots? The observance of Christmas among Christians in the West may have arisen in a similar way as a means of eliminating the observance of the Roman Saturnalia Festival which occurred in December. Whatever its origins may be, Purim has become a popular and joyous celebration of God's saving help for His people.

Channukah which occurs in December commemorates the rededication of the temple in Jerusalem following the Jews' successful revolt against the Syrian King Antiochus Epiphanes IV in the Second Century. The book of Macchabees records the fact that when they entered the temple, which had been profaned by idolatry, they discovered only enough oil to keep the temple lamp burning for a single day. Miraculously the oil lasted eight days, long enough for additional oil to be located. A special eight-stemmed *menorah* or candelabra is used as a symbol of this miracle, with one additional candle being lit successively on each of the eight nights of the festival. This Feast of Lights has become for Jews around the world a time to rekindle their spirit of

Menorah

patriotism and national pride. Because it is celebrated in December, in some countries there has been a tendency to adopt some of the Christmas customs: frequently Channukah lights are burned in the windows of Jewish homes, and gift-giving especially to children has become commonplace.

In additon to these major festivals there are several other minor ones as well, but for Jews everywhere the weekly celebration of *shabbat* or the sabbath is perhaps the most constant reminder of their faith in the God who created the world in six days, and rested on the seventh. The sabbath starts at sunset on Friday and ends at sunset on Saturday. Its observance begins with the lighting of the seven-stemmed menorah, followed by a festive evening meal shared by the members of a family. Some Jews attend a Friday evening service at the synagogue, and most do so on Saturday morning. As indicated earlier, Orthodox Jews keep the sabbath very strictly, avoiding all forms of physical exertion. In Israel today, where orthodox customs are the rule, the Sabbath is signaled in by the sounding of a siren. Shops and places of business all close. The hectic activity on the streets soon subsides, and, until the siren sounds again at sunset on Saturday, peace and tranquility prevail. In this way each Jew is reminded of the special relationship he enjoys with his God, the God of Abraham, of Isaac, and of Jacob—the God of Israel.

Review Questions

1. Defend the validity of this statement: "Unless one knows something of the history of the Jewish people, one will never truly understand Judaism."

2. Why is Judaism such an excellent example of the evolution of religious concepts?

3. Compare and contrast Judaism before and after the Exile. Why do scholars feel that this experience constituted a major turning-point for Judaism?

4. Briefly summarize the most important turning-points in Jewish history before the time of Christ. Select any one event and describe the impact that this experience had on the development of Judaism.

5. Briefly summarize the most important turning-points in Jewish history during the Christian era. Select any one event and describe the impact that this experience had on the development of Judaism.

6. Identify: covenant, Exodus, Babylonian Exile, diaspora, judges, prophets, First Temple, Second Temple, sanhedrin, the Macchabees, Antiochus Epiphanes IV, Theodosius, rabbi, synagogue worship, polygamy, anti-semitism, holocaust, barmitzvah, Zionism, Hasidism, kosher, sabbath, Torah, Talmud, menorah.

7. Distinguish clearly among the principal traditions within Judaism: orthodox, conservative, and reform. What other traditions exist?

8. What are the major festivals in Judaism? Describe their origins and the manner in which they are observed.

9. Briefly describe the background for the foundation of the State of Israel. Why is Israel so important to Jews all over the world?

Acknowledgements And Notes

Religions Of The East:

1. "The Sacred and the Profane" *The Sacred And The Profane* by Mircea
   Eliade, New York: Harcourt, Brace and Co., 1959. Introduction.
   (East-p. 4)

2. "Principles of Primitive Mythology" *Myth And Reality* by Mircea
   Eliade, New York: Harper and Row, 1963. pp. 18ff.
   (East-p. 4)

3. "Six Elements of Religion" *The Religions Of Man* by Huston Smith,
   New York: Harper & Row, 1958. pp. 101-108.
   (East-p. 27f)

4. "Mao Tse-Tung and Confucianism" (quote)—*China's New Democracy*
   by Mao Tse-Tung, New York: International, 1945. p. 48
   (East-p. 52)

5. "Hirohito's Denial of Divinity" (quote)—*The Long Search* by Ninian
   Smart, Boston: Little Brown and Co., 1977. p. 278.
   (East-p. 59)

Pictures

Bill Aron p. 103

Mimi Forsyth pp. 1, 13, 21, 23, 26, 30, 34, 42, 46

Algimantas Kezys p. 88

Religious News Service pp. 61, 70, 98

Unicorn Stock Photos p. 76

Visual Impressions pp. 19, 52, 57